TRANSACTIONAL ANALYSIS
COUNSELLING
IN ACTION

Third Edition

Ian Stewart

SAGE Publications
Los Angeles · London · New Delhi · Singapore

First published 1989
Reprinted 1991, 1992 (twice)
Second Edition first published 2000
Reprinted 2002, 2004, 2006 (twice)

SAGE Publications Ltd
1 Oliver's Yard
55 City Road
London EC1Y 1SP

SAGE Publications Inc.
2455 Teller Road
Thousand Oaks, California 91320

SAGE Publications India Pvt Ltd
B 1/I 1 Mohan Cooperative Industrial Area
Mathura Road, New Delhi 110 044
India

SAGE Publications Asia-Pacific Pte Ltd
33 Pekin Street #02-01
Far East Square
Singapore 048763

British Library Cataloguing in Publication data

A catalogue record for this book is available from the
British Library

ISBN 978-1-4129-3494-7
ISBN 978-1-4129-3495-4 (pbk)

Library of Congress Control Number: 2007923070

Typeset by C&M Digitals (P) Ltd, Chennai, India
Printed in Great Britain by The Cromwell Press Ltd, Trowbridge, Wiltshire
Printed on paper from sustainable resources

CONTENTS

PREFACE TO THE FIRST EDITION

This book is a practical guide to the use of transactional analysis (TA) in counselling and psychotherapy.

I have written primarily for the counsellor or counsellor-in-training whose background has been in a counselling method other than TA, and who is now interested in adding TA resources to her or his counselling skills. I hope the book will also be useful to counsellors and psychotherapists who are already practising or training professionally in TA.

What the Book Covers

This book is similar in its coverage to the other volumes in the *Counselling in Action* series:

- It focuses on practical application. Theory is covered only in so far as is essential for the understanding of practice, and then only in basic outline.
- The sequence of chapters reflects successive stages in the typical process of counselling with TA.
- The book deals with one-to-one counselling, not groupwork.
- It describes applications for use with people who are well-functioning in clinical terms, rather than those who might require psychiatric help.

This book is not intended to be a general introduction to TA. Present-day TA offers a multitude of explanatory models and at least three major schools of practice (Barnes, 1977). Rather than trying to cram a mass of detail into this practical guidebook, I have selected the areas of current TA that I believe have most to offer the practising counsellor. These I have covered in enough depth to do them justice.

TA began with Eric Berne, and his ideas still form the core of TA theory. Yet in the two decades since Berne's death, transactional analysts have continued to innovate. Much – probably most – of what TA practitioners do today depends on new theory and practice developed after Berne. You will find this new material emphasized in the content of this book.

There are two other aims that I have kept in mind in choosing topics:

- I have concentrated on theory and techniques that will be useful to you even if TA is not your main counselling approach.
- I have emphasized practical areas of TA that have not been easily accessible until now outside the specialist TA literature.

Indeed, the whole book is constructed around two linked concepts that are central to current practice in TA: *treatment direction* and *treatment sequence*. I believe these ideas have much to offer any practising counsellor. Yet, to my knowledge, this book marks the first systematic description of them other than in specialized workshop presentations.

This book is intended to be a resource for TA training, not a substitute for it. If you are interested in becoming professionally accredited in TA, you can obtain details of the necessary training and examination process from the various national and international TA organizations.

'Counselling' or 'Psychotherapy'?

Like anyone writing in this area, I have had to consider the problem of distinguishing between 'counselling' and 'psychotherapy'. It seems to me that while there may be sensible arguments for making a distinction between the two, any dividing line between them must in the end be drawn arbitrarily. And of the various arbitrary divisions that have been suggested, how was I to judge which to use?

My response in this book has been to draw no dividing line. The only restriction I have imposed on the book's coverage is to exclude applications designed for use with the more seriously troubled or with specialized client-groups. With that proviso, everything I say in this book applies to *all* professional relationships that have personal change as their aim, whether that work be labelled 'counselling' or 'psychotherapy'.

How the Book is Laid Out

In Part I, Chapter 1 presents some distinctive features of TA practice. Chapter 2 gives an overview of the counselling process in TA, from intake to termination. This also serves as a 'thumbnail sketch' of the structure of the remaining chapters, arranged as they are to reflect the sequence of steps in TA treatment. In Chapter 3 I outline the theory by which TA explains the origins and structure of personal problems. Chapter 4 explains the model of personality that is a foundation of TA theory and practice.

Part II moves on to a step-by-step description of the treatment process. Chapter 5 outlines typical TA procedure at intake. Chapter 6 describes how you can compile information about your client that you can use as the basis for a systematic treatment plan. In Chapter 7 I explain the procedure which transactional analysts have developed for monitoring and forestalling suicide risk.

Chapter 8 shows how you and your client can negotiate a clear contract for change. In Chapters 9 and 10 I describe detailed interventions by which you can help your client achieve that change. Lastly, Chapter 11 discusses criteria for termination.

In describing each aspect of TA practice, I have followed a standard (though flexible) sequence. Its steps are as follows:

- A basic outline of the theory underlying this area of practice. I usually present theory in the form of a 'Key Ideas' panel. This lists the central points of the relevant theory. They are phrased as brief statements. I make no attempt to expand the reasoning of the theory or to examine the detailed evidence on which it is based. (If you do wish to go more deeply into these questions, you can pursue the TA literature via the References list at the end of the book.)
- A discussion of the practical actions that follow from the theory. What is your rationale for making this assessment or this intervention? What are your purposes in doing so?
- A description of a specific technique or techniques.
- A case example to illustrate technique.
- A 'Self-supervision' sequence. This is a suggested checklist of questions that you can use, if you wish, in appraising your own work with clients. Each self-supervision is intended to help you sharpen your TA skills in the area of practice concerned.

You may wish to choose one client with whom you will follow through the successive steps in the process of counselling with TA. You can then apply the self-supervision exercises in sequence to your work with that client. If you choose not to do this, simply read 'a client' wherever I have written 'your chosen client' in the self-supervision panels.

Cases and Names

An extended case history runs through the book to illustrate practice and theory. The case of 'John' is based on that of a real client. However, I have disguised his story at some points. To do this I have inserted case material from work with other clients whose journeys were similar to John's. If I had given exact detail of John's case, there would have been a risk that he might be identified, even under a fictitious name.

At some points I have used examples from the work of other clients, collated in the same way as I have described for John.

In all the case examples, the names I use are fictitious. If they have any likeness to the real name of any person, this is purely by coincidence.

Pronouns and Genders

I use a simple system of pronouns throughout the book. You, the counsellor, are 'you'. I, Ian Stewart, am 'I'. Your client is either 'she' or 'he'. I vary your client's gender at random.

Thanks and Acknowledgements

I have drawn material for this book from the writing and teaching of hundreds of TA professionals. Whenever I knew whose work I was quoting, I have named her or him in the References list. There will be others whose ideas I have used without knowing their names. To all these contributors, named or anonymous, I am grateful.

There are a few people in particular whose work I draw upon time and time again throughout the book. They are master practitioners and teachers of TA. I have benefited from their writing, learned from them in workshops and supervision, and changed as their client in therapy. They are: Fanita English; Richard Erskine; Mary Goulding; Robert Goulding; Ken Mellor; Shea Schiff; Marilyn Zalcman. My thanks to them all.

Petrūska Clarkson was 'expert reader' for the book. In her comments on successive drafts, she gave me the benefit of her vast experience in TA and other fields of psychology and psychotherapy.

Dennis Bury commented on the manuscript from the viewpoint of an experienced counsellor using an approach other than TA. He helped me be aware of the importance of *apologia*: the need to write in ways that would be meaningful to people who viewed TA 'from the outside'.

Windy Dryden, series editor, is a master of motivation. Wielding both carrot and stick, Windy propelled me through one revision of the manuscript after another. He vetted every word of every re-write, always sensitive to the needs of the reader. This book is immeasurably better for his work.

I am grateful to the following authors for their permission to use copyright material originally published in the *Transactional Analysis Journal*, issues as shown:

- Richard Erskine and Marilyn Zalcman for 'The Racket System: A Model for Racket Analysis', *Transactional Analysis Journal* (1979) 9(1): 51–9.
- Ken Mellor and Eric Sigmund, for 'Discounting', *Transactional Analysis Journal* (1975) 5(3): 295–302.
- My thanks to Marilyn Zalcman also for her permission to use copyright material she presented in a workshop on 'Racket Analysis and the Racket System' at the EATA Conference, Noordwijkerhout, Holland, 1986. (This includes the use of the term *scripty fantasies*, and of the words *rage*, *terror*, *despair* and *ecstasy* to describe script feelings.)

I believe that a book can be a two-way communication, not simply a one-way vehicle. In writing this book I have had the pleasure of conveying ideas to you. I hope that as you read, you will convey your ideas back to me. If you have criticisms, compliments or comments, please send them to me via Sage Publications. Happy reading.

Ian Stewart
Nottingham, February 1989

PREFACE TO THE SECOND EDITION

In the Preface to the first edition of this book, I said that 'in the two decades since Berne's death, transactional analysts have continued to innovate'. Now the 'two decades' have become three, and transactional analysts are still innovating. The TA literature continues to expand, mirroring the expansion in the use of TA as a method of counselling and psychotherapy.

Yet during the past ten years, innovation in TA has seen a distinctive change in direction. The 'cutting edge' of new thought has moved on to more advanced and specialized areas of TA theory and practice, leaving the core concepts and basic techniques of TA essentially untouched. Perhaps this shift in emphasis is fitting for a mature discipline that has a documented history now going back more than forty years (Stewart, 1996b). TA theorists in the past decade have concentrated largely on comparative and cross-disciplinary issues (particularly, the relationships between TA theory and that of psychodynamic and object-relations approaches). Innovations in TA practice over the past ten years have focused on work with specific client-groups – notably on clients with borderline and narcissistic disorders, as well as on work with children and adult survivors of abuse. Both theory and practice have been codified, and TA now has its own *Dictionary* (Tilney, 1998).

My task of revision for this second edition, therefore, has been pleasantly easy. All the features of theory and practice covered in this book, drawn as they are from the well-established 'central core' of TA, remain as immediate and valid as they were ten years ago. The structure and content of the book thus stay essentially unchanged in this new edition.

Changes from the First Edition

The revisions in this second edition consist mainly of changes in wording, designed to clarify explanation or change emphasis. I thank the readers and reviewers of the first edition who suggested many of these revisions.

In particular, I have expanded the description of 'closing escape hatches' (Chapter 7) to emphasize that this procedure is always to be regarded as a crucial step in counselling, never as something to do 'as routine' or 'by rote'. In Chapter 4's account of ego-state theory, I have standardized the wording to bring out the point that each person has three *classes of* ego-state (Parent, Adult and Child) and not 'three ego-states'. I have re-worded the discussion of contract-making (Chapter 8) to fit the important realization that a contract can be *observable* without necessarily being 'behavioural'. There are other clarifications of wording throughout the book. I have, of course, updated the literature references.

How This Book Relates to *Developing TA Counselling*

My book *Developing Transactional Analysis Counselling* (Stewart, 1996a) offers thirty practical suggestions on how to enhance your effectiveness in TA counselling. In choosing the thirty suggestions, I followed the principle that I would not duplicate any of the material in the present book. Instead, *Developing TA Counselling* is designed to complement this book; in a sense, it 'starts where this book leaves off'. The present book lays down a solid groundwork for TA counselling, while *Developing TA Counselling* is more to do with fine-tuning and expanding your TA skills. At the same time, either book can be read on its own without loss of usefulness.

Where particular suggestions (called 'Points') in *Developing TA Counselling* are immediately relevant to topics covered in this book, you will find references to these Points in the boxes headed 'Further Reading in *Developing TA Counselling*' which I have added at the ends of the chapters concerned.

Once again, I wish you happy reading, and I hope this book will continue to be useful to you in the ten years to come.

Ian Stewart
Nottingham, May 1999

PREFACE TO THE THIRD EDITION

Seven years – rather than my predicted ten – have flown past, and here we are with the third edition of this book. Once again, just as in the ten years leading up to the second edition, transactional analysts have continued to innovate and expand the boundaries of the discipline. Yet once again also, the well-established core theory and techniques of TA, described here, have stayed virtually unchanged.

The structure and coverage of this book therefore remain essentially the same as in the two earlier editions. At the same time, this new edition contains some major revisions and additions.

Changes from the Second Edition

The most substantial changes are in the chapters in Part II that deal with the process of treatment, including contract-making. Already in the second edition, I had re-written Chapter 7, 'Blocking Tragic Outcomes', to underline the fact that the therapeutic process of 'closing escape hatches' should never be regarded as an operation that can simply be carried out 'as routine'. Yet, even in the months in which I have been preparing this third edition, I have encountered the 'urban myth' which still seems to be circulating among some TA trainees: the myth of 'rote escape-hatch closure'. In this edition, I have therefore re-written Chapter 7 yet again, using every device of language and typography I can think of, to specify the reality: there is no such thing as 'rote escape-hatch closure', because if the process is carried out by rote, then the client will almost certainly not close the escape hatches. I have also suggested some answers to the good question: 'If you don't invite hatch closure at the very beginning of counselling, then when *do* you invite it?'

In Chapter 8, on contract-making, I have also amplified some amendments that were first introduced in the second edition, to clarify the distinction between the terms 'behavioural' and 'observable' as applied to contracts in TA. I have rewritten the relevant section to make the distinction still clearer and explain more specifically why it is important. I have also added a new subsection to the list of features of an effective contract, namely that the contract goal should be set in a clear context.

I have re-written the section on 'Impasses' in Chapter 10, 'Making New Decisions', so that the description now consistently follows the theoretical model most often used by transactional analysts today, that of Ken Mellor (1980a), and have added some practical guidelines on distinguishing the three types of impasse one from another.

As well as these revisions, I have made changes in detail in every chapter, to clarify various points of explanation, add hints on practical application, and provide extra cross-referencing. Literature references have, of course, been updated.

Thanks and Acknowledgements

Mark Widdowson was invited by Sage to be the 'critical reviewer' for this third edition. Mark took a fine-tooth comb through the text of the second edition, and presented me with a detailed and perceptive list of suggested revisions. His suggestions, plus the thoughts and reflections they sparked off in my own mind, are the source of all the major changes that I have just outlined (and most of the minor changes, too). I thank Mark most heartily for his work. My thanks also go to the readers who have contacted me with suggestions for revision, and to my trainees, supervisees and clients, from whom I continue to learn.

New Thinking in TA Since 2000

While the area of innovation in TA in the 1990s was principally concerned with the diagnosis and treatment of specific client groups, the first decade of the twenty-first century has so far seen a shift in emphasis toward new thinking on the philosophy and meta-theory of transactional analysis. Much of this new literature has centred around what has come to be called the 'relational approach' to TA. This school of thought is a broad church, subsuming elements of constructivism (Allen and Allen, 1997), co-creative

TA (Summers and Tudor, 2000) and integrative psychotherapy (Moursund and Erskine, 2004). It emphasizes a rapprochement between TA and psychoanalysis (for example, Novellino, 2005).

If I may attempt to summarize the relational approach in a few sentences: it calls for an increased focus on unconscious processes, and on the manifestation of these processes in the transference and countertransference exchanges between therapist and client. In terms of the practice of TA, the relational approach sees the process of change as materializing from moment to moment in the therapist–client relationship, rather than as being a planned movement toward an agreed contractual goal. If you are interested in exploring the relational approach in detail, I would recommend the symposium volume *From Transactions to Relations* (Cornell and Hargaden, 2005) as a good starting point from which you can trace the literature on the subject.

Cornell and Hargaden (2005: 5) suggest that the relational approach constitutes a 'paradigm shift' that will redefine the discipline of TA. In my view, this claim probably overstates the case. I think it is more likely that when the dust settles, the relational approach will take its place as one of many useful perspectives on TA theory and practice, its main contribution being to remind us that the client–therapist relationship – conscious and unconscious – must always be considered alongside treatment planning and technique. Time will tell. It seems to me in any case that this area of innovation in TA, like the new thinking of the 1990s, still lies on the outer frontiers of the discipline. The books and articles so far published by the members of the relational school are aimed at advanced practitioners and theorists; I find it difficult to see them as practical 'how to' guides for immediate application by working counsellors, therapists or trainees. Nor do the ideas of the relational theorists detract from or contradict any of the well-established theory and practice described in the present book.

'Counselling' vs. 'Psychotherapy'

In the Preface to the first edition, I said that I regarded the distinction between 'counselling' and 'psychotherapy' as arbitrary, and that my response in this book was to make no distinction. I want to re-state that position here. Everything I say in this book about counselling can equally well be applied to psychotherapy.

I know that in some other European countries it is politically and legally important for colleagues to maintain a sharp distinction between the activities labelled 'counselling' and 'psychotherapy'. Luckily, in the UK we do not have to do this. On the contrary, since this book's second edition appeared, there has been a continuing movement to run the two labels together. Some 'straws in the wind': the former British Association for Counselling is now the British Association for Counselling and Psychotherapy. (And even before their name change, the BAC defined counselling as *including* psychotherapy – eminently sensibly, in my view). Sage's volume on contract-making, previously called *Contracts in Counselling,* has been re-badged for its second edition as *Contracts in Counselling and Psychotherapy* (Sills, 2006). Perhaps by the time the fourth edition of the present book appears, the entire series of *In Action* titles will have been re-named *Counselling and Psychotherapy in Action.* I hope so.

I should have liked to use the words 'counselling' and 'psychotherapy' interchangeably throughout the book, but did not get round to asking Windy Dryden about this in time for the print deadline. Therefore, I ask you to imagine I have done so. As it is, I have taken the liberty of retrospectively changing the first sentence in the Preface to the 1989 edition to say: 'This book is a practical guide to the use of transactional analysis in counselling *and psychotherapy.*' That was the book's purpose seventeen years ago, and it still is. I hope you continue to find it useful in this new, revised edition.

Ian Stewart
Nottingham, January 2007

Part I

THE TA FRAMEWORK

COUNSELLING WITH TA

This chapter gives you an overview of TA work and TA skills. In this first section I outline some distinctive features of TA practice. The second section discusses some personal and professional qualities of the effective counsellor.

Practice and Philosophy in TA

TA practice is founded on a set of philosophical views about people and the goals of change. The philosophical assumptions of TA can be summed up in three statements:

- People are OK.
- Everyone has the capacity to think.
- People decide their own destiny, and these decisions can be changed.

From these assumptions there follow two guiding principles of TA practice:

- contractual method
- open communication.

People are OK

Everyone has worth, value and dignity. This is a statement of essence rather than behaviour. At times, I may not esteem or accept what a person does. But always, I esteem and accept what he or she is.

In the counsellor–client relationship, this implies that you and your client are on an equal footing. Neither is one-up nor one-down to the other.

This assumption will be familiar to you if you know person-centred counselling, since it implies Rogers' 'unconditional positive regard' (Rogers, 1961: 62; Mearns and Thorne, 2007). The TA assumption also underlines the need for the counsellor to maintain unconditional positive regard for *himself* ('I'm OK') as well as for the client ('You're OK').

Everyone has the capacity to think

Everyone, except the severely brain-damaged, has the capacity to think. Therefore each person has the ability to decide what she wants from life. She carries ultimate responsibility for living with the consequences of her decisions.

Decisional model

Each person decides her own behaviour, thoughts and feelings, and ultimately her own destiny. No one can be *made* to act, think or feel in particular ways by other people or by the environment, except by physical coercion.

From this *decisional model* of human action follows TA's emphasis on *personal responsibility* for feeling, thought and behaviour.

The decisional model is also at the root of the theory of psychopathology in TA. The young child is viewed as *deciding* his or her responses to environmental pressures. This has implications for the process of personal change in adult life. Because dysfunctional patterns were originally decided upon, rather than being forced upon the individual, they can be changed by making new decisions.

Thus TA holds that people can change. This change can be genuine and lasting. Change is not brought about merely by achieving insight into old patterns. Rather, the person can actively decide to replace these patterns by new ways of behaving, thinking or feeling that are appropriate to her grown-up abilities.

Contractual method

From the assumptions that people relate as equals and that everyone is personally responsible, it follows that you and your client have joint responsibility for the process of change. To facilitate this, you enter into a *contract*. Your client states the goal he wants to achieve, and says what he is willing to do to help bring this about. You say whether you are willing to work with the client to achieve the chosen goal, and undertake to use the best of your professional skills when you do work together.

Open communication

In TA practice, you keep your case notes open to the client's inspection. This open communication helps your client take an equal role with you in the process of change.

Treatment Direction

The phrase *treatment direction* implies an informed choice of treatment procedures, decided upon in the light of psychodiagnosis and systematically followed through in the service of the contract goal. Current TA practice lays great importance on the need to choose and maintain direction in treatment.

Treatment planning is always a deliberate and explicit process for the TA practitioner. It includes decisions on *treatment sequence*, the order in which various stages of the treatment process will be carried out. There are certain steps which the transactional analyst will usually follow in sequence when carrying through his treatment plan. These stages of treatment will be described one by one in the successive chapters of Part II. Chapter 2 introduces this with a bird's-eye view of the typical treatment sequence.

Process Awareness: 'Thinking Martian'

TA stresses the need to stay aware of the *process* of communication as well as its content. That is, you need to pay attention to how people say things as well as to what they say.

Eric Berne urged TA practitioners to 'think Martian'. He pictured a little green man from Mars arriving on this planet to study Earthlings. The Martian has never been conditioned to accept what human communications *should* mean. He simply observes them and considers the results which follow. From this he deduces what these communications *do* mean. The practitioner, said Berne, needs to redevelop this skill of 'thinking Martian': observing human interaction without preconception. It is a skill every infant possesses naturally. As part of the process of growing up, most of us are systematically discouraged from using that skill ('It's rude to stare, dear!'), and we lose it through disuse.

In TA work you therefore re-learn to pay close attention to your client's non-verbal clues: breathing signals, bodily tensions, changes of posture. You observe these signals over short time-spans, since they change from one split second to the next.

You pay attention also to the person's choice of words. This is part of judging *how* things are said. For example, you would interpret the statement 'That makes me feel bad' as having a different meaning from 'I feel bad about that'. (I explain the difference in Chapter 9.) You will choose your own words with equally close attention.

Social level and psychological level

As part of 'thinking Martian', TA distinguishes two levels of communication: the *social level* and the *psychological level*. The idea behind this is that when people communicate, they often convey more than one message at the same time.

As illustration of this, consider the following exchange between counsellor and client:

> COUNSELLOR: So will you complete the assignment we've just agreed?
> CLIENT: [*Breaks eye contact, shakes head slightly*] Yes, I will.

Intuitively, you feel the client is communicating something more to the counsellor than the literal meaning of his words would indicate. The 'Key Ideas' box below sets out the ideas that TA uses to explain this kind of exchange. I shall illustrate each of them by this same example.

Key Ideas 1.1

SOCIAL-LEVEL AND PSYCHOLOGICAL-LEVEL MESSAGES

1 All communication proceeds at two levels: the *social level* and the *psychological level*.
2 The *social-level message* is the meaning of the communication as it is conventionally understood in the social circle of the people concerned. In our example, the client's social-level message is that he will complete the assignment.
3 The *psychological-level message* is the communication's real meaning, the 'Martian'. You will pick this up initially by intuitive judgement. Usually you will

follow up by asking the other person whether this judgement is accurate. The counsellor in the example might judge that his client's 'Martian' is conveying 'No, I won't do it' or 'I'm very doubtful if I'll do it'.

4   Often, but not always, the social-level message is conveyed in the literal meaning of the words and the psychological-level message is conveyed by non-verbal signals. In our example, the client's headshake and breaking of eye contact signal the psychological-level message.

5   If the social level and psychological level convey the same message, the two levels are said to be *congruent*. This is not so in our example. To make his messages congruent, the client might have maintained eye contact with the counsellor and made a slight nod of the head instead of shaking it.

6   If the message conveyed on the psychological level is different from that conveyed on the social level, there is said to be *incongruity* between the two levels, and the psychological-level message is said to be *ulterior*. In the example, the client's headshake belied his agreement to doing the assignment, and thus was a signal of incongruity. The possible ulterior messages conveyed by the incongruity have been suggested in (3) above.

7   The behavioural outcome of any communication is determined at the psychological and not at the social level.

Eric Berne (1966: 227) put forward statement 7 above as a 'rule of communication'. You will note that he wrote 'is determined', not 'may be determined'. Berne is asserting that the psychological-level message is *always* the 'real message' in this sense. In our example, this is to say: if the counsellor wants to know what the client really means by his communication, he should pay attention to the client's ulterior message and not his social-level message.

At first sight it may seem too sweeping to claim that the outcome of communication is *always* decided at the psychological level. Yet researchers into body language in fields other than TA are familiar with the notion of 'non-verbal leakage' (for example, Scheflen, 1972). Implicit in this idea is that the non-verbal signals do indeed always convey what is 'really going on'.

'Overt' vs. 'covert' messages

It may seem at first sight that the social-level message is 'overt' while the psychological-level message is 'covert'. In fact, both levels are overt. The psychological-level message only appears 'covert' if you view it from within the conventional social framework of what a communication is 'supposed to' mean. This in turn demands that you blank out your awareness of non-verbal signalling, as most of us are taught to do during childhood.

There are occasions when the psychological-level message is overt even in the literal meaning of the words. Example:

COUNSELLOR: So will you complete the assignment we've just agreed?
CLIENT: Yes, I'll try to.

In TA practice you would assume here that your client's real message is accurately conveyed by what he says. He will try to complete the assignment. But he will not actually complete it, because if he did, he would not be 'trying to' any more. This message only appears 'covert' if you interpret the words in terms of what they are conventionally 'supposed to' mean in everyday conversation.

In cases like this, the presence of the double message is signalled by the fact that your client has not actually answered the question you asked. (You enquired if he was going to do the assignment, not if he was going to try to do it.) I expand this topic in Chapter 9.

The Effective Counsellor

The TA practitioner, said Eric Berne, needs to be a 'real doctor'. Berne was not suggesting that only medical doctors should become transactional analysts. He meant that the TA professional must be prepared to take on certain responsibilities expected of a medical doctor (Berne, 1966: xvii). The 'real doctor', said Berne, must:

- be oriented first and foremost towards curing his patients
- be able to plan his treatment so that at each phase he knows what he is doing and why he is doing it
- take sole responsibility for his patients' welfare within the area of his professional competence.

Permission, Protection and Potency

Crossman (1966) has suggested 'three Ps' which the effective practitioner must bring to her counselling work. They are *permission, protection and potency*.

Permission

To offer someone *permission*, you provide her with new messages about herself, others and the world. These messages realistically describe the person's grown-up resources and options. She can use them to replace old restrictive or destructive messages that she may have perceived her parents as giving her in childhood. Examples:

'You do have the power to think and make decisions.'
'You are valuable and lovable.'
'You *can* survive and get your needs met even if you don't work hard all the time.'
'As a grown-up person, you will survive even without your parents' support.'

If you choose, you may convey permissions to your client in words. But more important is that you yourself must *model the permissions congruently*. That is, what you do must match what you say. Or to put this in the language we used in the 'Key Ideas' panel above: to be congruent, you must convey the same message at both social level and psychological level.

For example, suppose you want to convey the permission 'You have the power to think clearly'. If you like, you may say this in words to your client. With or without the words, she is most likely to take the permission if you show in your behaviour that you fully believe she can think clearly. One way to model this would be to invite her consistently to think for herself. You would avoid any temptation you might feel to try to 'think for her'. For instance, if you asked her a question and she acted confused, you would not fill in the answer for her. Instead you would wait for her to find her own answer. Another element of modelling would be for you to show her that you can think clearly yourself.

To be congruent in modelling permissions for your client, *you yourself must already have taken the permissions you are modelling*.

Protection and potency

If the client does take new permissions, he will be going against directives that he perceived his parents laying down for him during his childhood. Outside of awareness the client may experience this change as risky, even life-threatening (Chapter 6). He may fear that he will lose the support of his internalized parent, bringing about some catastrophe such as extinction or abandonment. Thus, without being fully aware of it, he may look to you for *protection* against this fantasized disaster. This requires also that he perceives you as having enough *potency* – enough power – to provide the needed support and protection.

For example, suppose you are working with a client who wants to be more free in showing his feelings. You thus offer him the permission 'It's OK to show your feelings in ways that are safe for you as a grown-up person.' But suppose also that this client decided in infancy 'If I show my feelings, my mother will leave me and never come back, so I'll die.' Without awareness, he may still be clinging to this infant motivation for concealing his feelings. If he is to make use of the new message you are offering, the young child part of him must first be convinced you can protect him against being abandoned and dying. And he can only achieve this conviction if that same child part of him sees you as having the power to offer the needed protection.

Protection and potency, like permission, are conveyed first and foremost by congruent modelling. You must be confident that you do possess more power than the client's fantasized parent. You must feel secure in your ability to protect and support the client during the process of change.

As well as this internal confidence, potency and protection are exhibited in the way you work. The potent counsellor is one who knows what she is doing and why she is doing it. This quality will be shown by the economy and appositeness of her interventions.

As one element of protection, TA lays much emphasis on forestalling three tragic outcomes. They are: killing or harming self, killing or harming others, or going crazy. In Chapter 7 we shall look at this protective process of 'closing the escape hatches'.

Protection for the client also means you must provide a physically safe environment. For example, if the session is likely to entail a physical release of anger, you give protection by setting up the room so that neither the client nor yourself can get hurt during the process. Two other essential ingredients of protection are confidentiality and an effective system for medical and psychiatric referral (Chapter 5).

To ensure competent decisions on referral, you need to have a working knowledge of some topics on the interface between your own practice and other fields. These areas of knowledge include:

- child development
- principal current theories of psychology and behaviour
- general physiology and biochemistry
- diagnosis of organic disorders or substance abuse
- the effects of medication and physical treatments
- general psychodiagnosis, including the use of standard diagnostic manuals
- legal issues in the area of counselling.

Counselling and Supervision for the Counsellor

You need to resolve your own therapeutic issues if you are to be fully effective as a counsellor. This is because congruent modelling is so important in conveying the 'three Ps'. You can only help your client achieve a particular goal to the same extent as you yourself have achieved it.

It follows that you need to enter counselling or psychotherapy yourself whenever you become aware of unresolved personal problems. To be fully effective with a wide range of clients, you need to be willing to resolve a correspondingly wide range of your own personal issues. If you become aware of a personal problem you have still not resolved and which you are putting in the way of your work with a given client, you need to refer that client to another counsellor.

Equally important is to be in on-going supervision. Since you are using the TA model, this will ideally be with an accredited TA supervisor. In this book, I have provided you with 'self-supervision' sequences, and self-supervision is indeed a useful tool: it helps you to stand back from your work and reflect on it 'from the outside'. By doing this, you can often pick out points where you could have intervened differently or more effectively. You may well become aware of 'blind spots' in your own awareness that you did not notice while you were actually working with the client.

But work with a supervisor gives you the extra benefit of another pair of eyes, which see your work from a different perspective. Importantly, this often enables the supervisor to pick up and reflect back to you any 'blind spots' in your perception that you did not notice, even during self-supervision. (We shall discuss these 'blind spots' in detail in Chapter 9, where we look at the TA concepts of *redefining* and *discounting*.) Another obvious benefit of supervision is that, unless you are already a highly experienced counsellor, the supervisor can advise you on the specifics of technique and treatment planning, drawing on her or his own experience. Supervision helps you avoid 're-inventing the wheel'.

In the next chapter, I give an overview of the successive stages that make up the typical process of treatment in TA. My own image of this sequence is that it resembles building a house. First you put in solid foundations. Then you start with the bottom bricks and work upwards. The soundness of the whole structure depends on how well you have laid the foundations and the bottom bricks.

I believe that this sequence describes not only the order of effective treatment, but also the best order in which you can build up your own TA skills. By achieving fluency in each successive aspect of the treatment sequence, you lay a sound foundation for developing skill in the stage that follows.

Further Reading in *Developing TA Counselling*

The 'Afterword' in *Developing TA Counselling* (Stewart, 1996a) further explores the concept of 'personal OKness' and its practical application in counselling.

2

PLANNING THE ROUTE TO CHANGE

Treatment Direction
Treatment Sequence
Further Reading in *Developing TA Counselling*

Treatment planning begins at your first contact with your client, and extends to the end of the counselling relationship. Its purpose is to ensure that, in Berne's phrase, 'at every stage you know what you are doing and why you are doing it'.

Effective treatment planning calls for decisions on *treatment direction*. In turn, treatment direction entails determining a *treatment sequence*. I explain these ideas in the sections that follow.

Treatment Direction

In TA work there is always a three-way interplay between your choice of interventions, the treatment contract you have agreed with your client, and your diagnosis of the client. This leads to the concept of *treatment direction*.

Key Ideas 2.1

TREATMENT DIRECTION

1 *Treatment direction* means the informed choice of interventions to facilitate the client in achieving the agreed *contract*, in the light of your *diagnosis* of the client.

2   Choice of interventions means choosing *which* interventions to use and *in what order* to use them.
3   In choosing which interventions to use, you need to consider both *content* and *process*: what you do and how you do it.
4   In choosing the order of your interventions, you are deciding *treatment sequence.*

To review the basic notion of *contract-making* in TA, see Chapter 1, under the heading *Practice and Philosophy in TA*. You will find a full discussion of contract-making techniques in Chapter 8.

The Treatment Triangle

I call Figure 2.1 the 'Treatment Triangle'. It pictures the three-way relationship between diagnosis, contract and treatment direction. (Figure developed by the author from a presentation by Guichard, 1987.) The whole diagram taken together represents the overall treatment plan.

The Role of Psychodiagnosis in TA

In this practical guidebook, I do not think it is useful to embark on debates about the pros and cons of psychodiagnosis. In any case, the argument has been thoroughly explored in other sources. (See, for example, Rowan, 1981; Szasz, 1961; Zigler and Phillips, 1961. For a review from a TA standpoint, see Clarkson, 1987 and 1992: 55–74.)

I will simply say that most transactional analysts regard psychodiagnosis as being central to effective treatment planning. The Treatment Triangle underlines how diagnosis is related both to the contract and to your decisions on treatment direction. The contract defines the aim of treatment. Diagnosis tells you where you and your client start from on your way towards this aim. Treatment direction means choosing what interventions to use, and in what order. Diagnosis gives you guidance to these choices, in ways that I shall describe in coming chapters.

Opponents of psychodiagnosis have complained that it entails 'labelling people'. The majority view in TA would be, rather, that diagnosis means labelling some things that people *do*. Each diagnostic 'label' denotes a particular set of signs and symptoms. Experience has suggested that certain modes of treatment are relatively effective when working with a

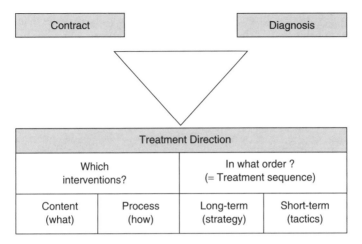

Figure 2.1   The Treatment Triangle

person showing these signs and symptoms, others relatively ineffective. Thus if you can determine the appropriate diagnostic label, you can move straight away to an avenue of treatment that is likely to be effective. You do not have to re-invent the wheel each time you take on a new client.

In TA practice an initial diagnosis may often be revised as the counsellor becomes better acquainted with the client. The frequent review of diagnosis is an integral part of treatment planning.

As the client achieves personal change in counselling, the appropriate diagnosis may also change.

Methods of diagnosis in TA

Diagnosis in TA practice does not only entail the use of a standard diagnostic manual, though this is part of the process. The counsellor will typically also employ various diagnostic models drawn from a TA framework. The aim is not simply to attach a diagnostic label. Rather it is to assemble a wide range of information about the client that will give detailed guidance to treatment planning.

As a current standard manual for diagnosis, transactional analysts routinely use the DSM-IV-TR (American Psychiatric Association, 2000). An important purpose of the standard diagnosis is to provide a common language for communication between the counsellor and her medical colleagues. The manual of choice, therefore, will be the one in use by psychiatric professionals in the counsellor's area.

Two TA models often used in diagnosis are fully explained in later chapters of this book. They not only serve a diagnostic function, but also provide specific guidance to intervention. They are:

- the Racket System (Chapters 3 and 6)
- the Discount Matrix (Chapter 9).

Treatment Sequence

The rationale of *treatment sequence* is that there are stages in treatment that need to be addressed in a particular order. If you omit one or more of these stages, or tackle them out of order, then the effectiveness of treatment may be diminished (Boyd, 1976; Clarkson, 1992: 90–147; Erskine, 1973; Pulleyblank and McCormick, 1985; Stewart, 1996a: 34–8; Ware, 1983; Woollams and Brown, 1978).

The Overall Treatment Sequence: First Contact to Termination

I have drawn Figure 2.2 in the form of a flow-chart. It summarizes the typical stages of the overall treatment sequence. I suggest that, at this early stage in the book, you simply scan the flow-chart to get an initial picture of treatment sequence. As you read through coming chapters, you may wish to refer back to this diagram to review how the various steps in treatment fit together. Figure 2.2 contains 'pointers' to show the chapters of this book in which each topic will be discussed in detail.

To fill out the technical information in Figure 2.2, here is a summary of the various stages in everyday language:

- INTAKE: deciding if it's OK to make the journey together.
- ASSESSMENT: finding out where the other person has come from.
- TREATMENT CONTRACT: discovering where she wants to get to, and deciding if you want to go there with her.
- TREATMENT DIRECTION: deciding a good way to get there.
- INTERVENTIONS: getting from here to there.
- TERMINATION: saying goodbye when you've finished the journey.

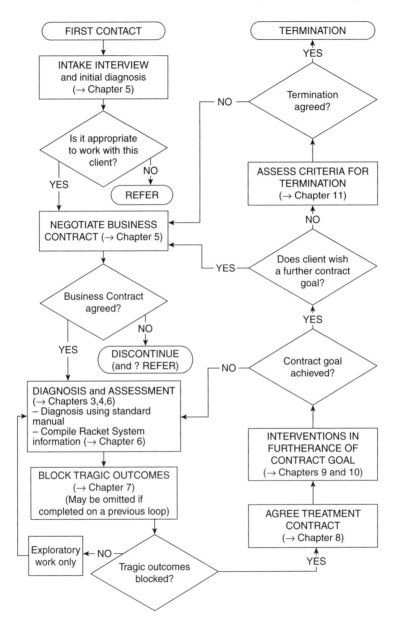

Figure 2.2   Flow-Chart of the Treatment Sequence

Treatment Planning as a Feedback Process

The loop structure of Figure 2.2 emphasizes the importance of *feedback* in treatment planning. At each stage of treatment, the results of previous stages provide feedback into the treatment plan. For instance, you may often find that you revise your initial assessment of the client as you gain new evidence from her responses to your interventions. In response you may re-write aspects of your treatment plan. As you make these changes it may become appropriate to negotiate a new contract goal. In turn, this may mean further changes in the strategy of your interventions.

Each time your client achieves one of the contract goals you and she have agreed, you have the joint choice whether to go on to agree a further treatment contract. If you do, you will re-enter the loop by re-negotiating your business contract if necessary, then reviewing the diagnosis. If not, you will move to termination.

Flexibility in the treatment plan

Figure 2.2 makes the process of treatment planning seem more mechanical than it usually is in practice. Once you have become familiar with the sequence, you can allow it to flow more freely. You can use your judgement in omitting stages or running them together. For example, you may not always carry out a formal re-assessment of your diagnosis every time your client achieves a contract goal. Rather, reviewing the diagnosis becomes an integral and almost instinctive part of your thinking about how to proceed with this client from one session to the next.

The stages of assessment and intervention are likewise closely related. They often flow together rather than happening in sequence. For example, you may spend several sessions with your client exploring the past patterns of beliefs, behaviours and feelings by which she has been setting up painful outcomes for herself. In the process of mapping these patterns, the client may become clearly aware of them for the first time. This awareness may itself be the first step in active change. The stages of 'Blocking Tragic Outcomes' and 'Agreeing Treatment Contract' may overlap or be reversed in the order of treatment.

There is also great scope for flexibility in the timescale of the various stages of the treatment sequence. Again this is difficult to show in a diagram. One way is to visualize the linking arrows in Figure 2.2 as being made of stretchy elastic. For example, with some clients you will move rapidly to a treatment contract and then spend many sessions on detailed interventions. With others, you may take months to work out what contract they want, but the establishment of the contract will itself be the main move the client needs to make. The entire treatment sequence might conceivably be fitted within one counselling session. At the other extreme, counselling may continue for several years.

You now have a ground-plan of TA's typical treatment sequence. We can next go on to look at the theory that underlies it. How does TA explain personal problems and the process of personal change?

Further Reading in *Developing TA Counselling*

Points 1, 2 and 3 in *Developing TA Counselling* (Stewart, 1996a) suggest some basic principles and techniques to aid your effectiveness in treatment planning.

3

MAPPING THE STRUCTURE OF PROBLEMS

Like most other therapeutic approaches, TA takes the view that many personal problems originate in childhood. However, TA has its own distinctive account of how this takes place. TA theory in this area centres on the concept of *life-script*: a personal life-story that each of us writes in childhood. In this chapter I cover four main topics:

* The nature and origins of life-script.
* The strategies people develop in childhood to gain attention from others.
* How the person may maintain these childhood strategies in adult life, even though they have become painful or self-limiting for her.
* How you can use this knowledge to plan effective interventions.

Key Ideas 3.1

MOTIVATION AND BEHAVIOUR: BASIC ASSUMPTIONS

1 *All* behaviours represent strategies for surviving and getting needs met.
2 If a person's behaviour produces painful or counter-productive results for him, this may be:

- because he is uninformed or misinformed about the consequences of the behaviour; or
- because, without awareness, he is replaying outdated childhood strategies. As a child he perceived these strategies as the best option for surviving and getting needs met. However, they are inappropriate to his present situation as an adult.

Counselling vs. coaching

Where someone's problems arise from being uninformed or misinformed, the initial treatment of choice is *coaching* – that is, helping them find the required information – rather than *counselling*. (I am using the word 'coaching' here in its usual dictionary sense, rather than in its more recent, specialized sense of 'business coaching'.) For example, suppose someone comes to you asking for counselling to help him overcome obesity. You discover the person has no idea of the calorific content of foods, the effect of exercise and so on. Your initial intervention may be to specify a good book on these topics and suggest that the person reads it. Similarly, if someone comes complaining of difficulty in talking to people, your starting point might be to suggest she attends a training course in conversational skills. Generally speaking, it is a good idea to check whether the client is uninformed or misinformed before taking a contract for counselling.

Of course, there is no sharp dividing line between coaching and counselling. Nor is it usually an 'either/or' situation: a personal problem will often be traceable partly to misinformation, partly to the use of outdated childhood strategies. Thus you will respond by using a combination of coaching and counselling. In the remainder of this book, I deal with the counselling element. This is what you will use when you and your client are dealing with questions of *life-script*.

Life-script

Beginning in earliest childhood, each person decides upon a plan for her life. This plan is known as the *life-script* (Berne, 1972; Steiner, 1974; Stewart and Joines, 1987: 99–169). Often, we simply use the term *script*.

The life-script is constructed in the form of a drama, with a clear-cut beginning, middle and end. The closing scene of the script is called the *script payoff*.

In adult life the person may play out parts of her infant life-plan. She does this without being consciously aware of it. At such times she is said to be *in script*, or to be engaging in *scripty* behaviours, thoughts or feelings.

Early Decisions

The young child's life-plan is not determined solely by external forces, by the parents or by the environment. Instead, the child *decides* on the life-script as a response to these external pressures. To express this idea, we say that life-script is *decisional*. It follows that two children exposed to the same environmental pressures may compose different life-scripts in response.

In script theory, the word *decision* is used in a specialized sense, different from its usual dictionary meaning. The child's early decisions are not made in the deliberate thinking way usually associated with adult decision-making. Instead, they are made non-verbally, in the form of emotional responses. They may also be reflected in the person's body as held physical tensions.

This idea of 'making decisions without words' may seem strange if you have not met it before. You will find examples and further explanation of this process later in the present chapter, when we discuss how early decisions fit into the model known as the Racket System, and in Chapter 6, in the section where we look at the formation of script beliefs in early childhood.

For now, here is a metaphor to help convey this idea. Suppose a cat is ill-treated by a particular tall man. That cat is very likely, from that time onward, to shy away from contact with *all* tall men. Imagine you are that cat. You are a smart animal, but you don't 'do' words. Now, in your own mind, 'turn off words', so that you are thinking as that cat does. Be the cat, and be aware – without words – of what you have decided about tall men. How do you know you have decided it?

Script Messages

Though the parents cannot dictate the child's script decisions, they can exert a strong influence upon them. They do so by conveying *script messages* to their children. These messages may be conveyed verbally or non-verbally. The non-verbal messages, conveyed earlier in the child's life, are likely to underlie the person's most fundamental script decisions.

Script messages may take the form of *commands*, for example, 'Drop dead!', 'Don't get close to people.' Alternatively they may be given as *attributions*, that is, statements about what the child is. An attribution may be said to the child directly ('You're stupid!') or passed on as a statement made about the child to a third party ('Little Jean isn't strong, you know'). Both these kinds of message may be accompanied by an element of *modelling* on the part of one or both parents. For example, a mother who never allows herself to be angry with her children may be modelling for them the script message 'Don't show anger'.

Origins of Script

The infant decides upon a life-script as a best strategy for surviving and getting needs met in a world that often seems hostile (Woollams, 1977). The young child is small and physically vulnerable. In her earliest infancy, she accurately perceives her parents as holding the power of life and death over her. Later, as a toddler, she is aware that she will probably survive her parents' anger or temporary absence. But she still experiences the parents as having power to satisfy her needs or leave them unsatisfied. She also sees them as defining reality: to her, what her parents say must necessarily be true.

The infant experiences emotions differently from an adult, and uses a different form of reality-testing (see, for example, Erikson, 1950; Piaget, 1951). It is on this basis that early decisions are made. The young child's emotional experience is of rage, despair, terror or ecstasy (Zalcman, 1986). She also does not have the adult's understanding of time. Thus, for example, when Mother is absent for a while the infant may conclude: 'Mother has gone away, and maybe she'll never be back. And that means I'm going to be left alone for ever and ever.' With this perception go emotions of terror, desolation and rage at Mother for her act of abandonment.

With an infant's concrete and magical thinking, the child may go on to 'make sense' of what has happened by deciding without words: 'Mother has gone away and left me. That must mean there's something wrong with me, though Mother isn't telling me what it is.' With this, the child makes a tentative script decision. This sequence may have to be repeated many times before the child arrives at the firm conclusion that there is, indeed, something the matter with her.

Although most early decisions are made through repetition, a child may sometimes make a script decision in response to one single, usually traumatic, incident. A client of mine, Maria, recalled how, as a small child during the Second World War, she and her sister had hidden in a cupboard upstairs in their house while enemy soldiers smashed their way through the rooms below. At that point, Maria had made the decision: 'I have to stay quiet and hidden, or something dreadful will happen.'

Three Tragic Script Outcomes

When the young child is composing her life-script, she may decide that it is to have a tragic ending. There are three possible tragic outcomes to the script:

• killing or harming self
• killing or harming others
• going crazy.

In Chapter 6 I shall say more about how the infant may come to decide upon such a disastrous closing scene for her life-story. In fact, most people who decide upon a tragic outcome never carry it out. But they may spend much of their lives engaging in various kinds of self-limitation that they perceive outside of awareness as defences against suicide, murder or going crazy.

Current TA practice thus lays much importance on forestalling these tragic outcomes as an essential step in personal change. The rationale and technique for doing this are explained in Chapter 7.

Life-script and life course

Tragic or otherwise, the closing scene of the script is not seen as being pre-determined. Berne (1972) distinguished the life-script – the life-story planned by the person in infancy – from the *life course*, that is, what actually happens. He suggested that the life course is the resultant of four interacting influences:

• heredity
• external events
• life-script
• autonomous decisions.

The last-named are decisions the person makes in the here-and-now with her full adult powers of action, feeling and thinking. They may include decisions for change which she makes during counselling.

Strokes and Stroke-seeking

In talking about the life-script so far, I have said that it represents child-hood strategies for 'surviving and getting needs met'. The most basic of these infant survival needs are food and drink, shelter and the presence of the caretaker. Close on the heels of these, however, comes the need for *stimulation* and contact with others.

In his formulation of TA theory, Berne (1961) emphasized the importance of this *stimulus-hunger* as a developmental need. He cited the work of researchers such as Spitz (1945) and Levine (1960). For the infant, an important source of stimulation is physical touching by the caretaker – literally, stroking. Berne extended the term *stroking* to mean not only physical touching, but any form of recognition extended by one person to another. In adult life, he suggested, we still need strokes, though we learn to accept them in symbolic as well as literal form.

If you are coming to TA with a background in another counselling modality, you may already have connected Berne's concept of 'stroking' with the human need for *attachment*, stressed in particular by Bowlby (1969) as well as by several writers from the object-relations school (cf. Klein, 1987). For these theorists, as for Berne, the need for attachment is first felt in infancy but continues to be a crucial motivation throughout adult life.

Key Ideas 3.2

STROKING

1 *Stimulus-hunger* is the need for stimulation and contact with others. It is a central developmental need for the infant.

2 The infant therefore works out strategies designed to keep up the supply of attention and stimulation she receives from others (colloquially, her supply of *strokes*).

3 In adult life, people still need strokes. They learn to accept strokes in symbolic form (as words or gestures) as well as through physical touching.

4 When under stress in adulthood, the person may revert without awareness to the stroke-seeking strategies she used in infancy. At such times, she has moved into script.

Positive and negative strokes

Strokes are traditionally classified as either *positive* or *negative*:

- A *positive stroke* is one that the giver of the stroke intends to be pleasurable to the person who receives it.

* A *negative stroke* is one that the giver of the stroke intends as unpleasant or unwelcome to the person who receives it.

Either type of stroke may be given verbally or non-verbally.

Why People May Seek Negative Strokes

In your counselling experience you will have noted how some people seem to set up time and again for painful things to happen to them. Different counselling approaches have different ways of accounting for this paradoxical behaviour. TA explains it in terms of strokes and the life-script.

No parent, no matter how loving, can provide the infant with all the positive strokes she demands. There will always be occasions when, from the young child's perspective, it seems frighteningly possible that the supply of strokes may dry up. She experiences this literally as a matter of life and death. Therefore every child develops strategies for extorting strokes from her caretakers. She continually tests out and refines these strategies, learning which of them most often get results in her family.

One thing the infant soon discovers is that when positive strokes seem to be running out, there are many things he can do to get a harvest of negative strokes in their place. When Mother seems reluctant to hold him, he can throw a tantrum. Then she does pay him some attention, even if it is by scowling and speaking harshly to him. The infant is satisfying his inborn need for stimulation, though his means of doing so are painful to him. Without conscious reasoning, he is following a simple principle: '*Any stroke is better than no stroke at all*' (Stewart and Joines, 1987: 73). Here again, we can express this in the language of attachment: better to stay attached, even if that attachment is painful, than to face the dreadful prospect of abandonment.

When this infant becomes an adult, he may at times go into script. When he does he will replay the same childhood strategy. Outside of awareness, he becomes scared in case his supply of strokes is going to run out. Yet he holds the belief that positive strokes are hard to come by. He responds by setting up situations in which others are likely to offer him plentiful negative strokes.

By the time he reaches adult life, he is no longer aware of how he sets up these situations, or of his infant motivation for doing so. Thus each time he reaches a painful outcome and reaps his negative strokes, he wonders how he has managed to get into this situation again. This is the basis of many of the repeating painful patterns that TA calls *games* (see Chapters 6 and 9).

Strokes as Reinforcement

Behaviour is often intended to attract strokes. Thus when that behaviour does attract the wanted strokes, the person will be more likely to repeat the same behaviour in future. In that sense we can say that stroking reinforces the behaviour that is stroked.

Since people may sometimes seek negative strokes as well as positive ones, it follows that they may choose behaviours that are likely to gain them negative as well as positive responses.

Stroking invites reinforcement not only of behaviours, but also of the life-script. Suppose a person replays a script belief, and that he behaves, thinks or feels in some way that expresses that belief. If others then stroke the person in response to these behaviours, thoughts or feelings, he is likely to construe their strokes as 'confirming' his script beliefs. Thus he comes to hold those script beliefs more strongly than before.

In the final section of this chapter, I shall discuss how you can use stroking in a directed manner to facilitate change in counselling.

How the Life-script is Maintained

As adults, we have left the original process of script-formation behind in our past. Yet we carry our script with us in the present. Usually we are not aware we are doing so. At times of pressure, we may revert to our old strategies. Unfortunately, these may sometimes be self-limiting or painful for us in our adult circumstances.

Key Ideas 3.3

HOW THE LIFE-SCRIPT IS MAINTAINED

1   The script *decisions* made in childhood are carried into adulthood as script *beliefs*.
2   In the course of growing up, the script beliefs are repressed from conscious awareness.
3   When under stress as an adult, the person may replay the script beliefs outside of awareness. At such times she is said to be *in script*.
4   When in script, the person responds to stress in the here-and-now by re-enacting her childhood strategies.

5   These strategies are likely to bring the same results as they brought in childhood.
6   The person, outside of awareness, perceives these outcomes as 'confirming' the script beliefs. Thus each time this process is repeated, she comes to hold her script beliefs more strongly than before.

The Racket System

To explain the process by which script is maintained, Richard Erskine and Marilyn Zalcman (1979) have developed a model known as the *Racket System*. It is shown in Figure 3.1. The diagram illustrates the way in which the person, when in script, enters a closed, self-perpetuating system of beliefs, actions and perceptions.

The word 'racket' here is used in a technical sense. It indicates a repetitive pattern of behaviours, thoughts and feelings that the person engages in while in script. A explanation of rackets will be given below and in Chapters 6 and 9.

Erskine and Moursund (1988) employ an amended version of the same model, calling it the *Script System*.

Script Beliefs and Feelings

The left-hand column in Figure 3.1 shows the person's script beliefs about self, others and the quality of life. Each script belief will reflect a script decision that the person made in childhood.

Erskine and Zalcman see script decisions as reflecting the infant's attempts to 'make sense of' unmet needs and unfinished feelings. For every infant, there are times when the expression of feelings does not bring the hoped-for response from the caretaker. When this happens over a period, the infant is likely to use *cognitive mediation* to alleviate the discomfort of the unmet need. That is, he finds a means of 'explaining away' the fact that his needs are not being met. He then uses this 'explanation' to make himself feel better temporarily. As grown-ups, we all frequently use this same means of looking after ourselves. But the young child arrives at his 'explanation' non-verbally, using the magical thinking typical of infancy.

Example: suppose the infant repeatedly reaches out for physical contact with mother, but she does not give it. The child experiences terror at the

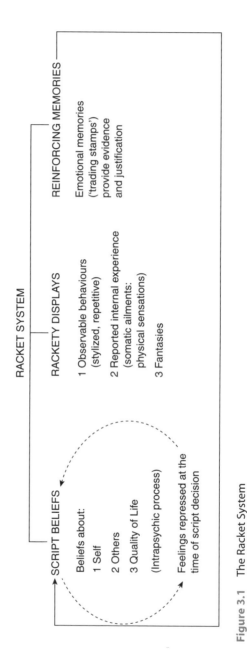

Figure 3.1 The Racket System

possibility of abandonment (Zalcman, 1986). He escalates the expression of this feeling by screaming, but still mother does not respond. Eventually the child runs out of energy and ceases screaming. He is left with his original need unmet and with his emotional experience unfinished.

To relieve at least some of the discomfort of this situation, the child may 'explain it away' by concluding without words 'I am unlovable'. If reinforced over a period of time, this would become one of the child's fundamental beliefs about himself. At a later stage of development, the child might elaborate his 'explanation' by adding the belief: 'The reason I'm unlovable is that there is something seriously the matter with me.'

This 'explanation' also implies for the infant that it is useless for him to continue expressing his original feeling. No matter how much he escalated, he still did not get his needs met. He responds by repressing the original feeling. That is, he decides not even to feel it. This repressed feeling is shown also in the left-hand column of the Racket System (Figure 3.1).

Now suppose that in adulthood the person meets a stress situation that in some way resembles the situation at the time of his script decision. In our example, this might be a perceived physical rejection by an important woman. Though he is not consciously aware of the connection, the person may re-contact memories of the traumatic rejection he experienced from his mother when he was an infant. He may respond to this memory by beginning to re-experience the terror he felt at the time. This emotion, like the memory with which it is connected, will be outside of his conscious awareness.

As he begins to re-experience this acute discomfort, the person attempts to deal with it in the same way as he did when he was an infant. He internally re-states his script beliefs in a renewed attempt to 'explain' to himself how he feels. In this example, the grown man might tell himself outside of awareness: 'Yes, it's just as I thought. All important women do reject me. That confirms that I'm unlovable, and that must be because there's something seriously the matter with me.'

By thus replaying his script beliefs, he 'justifies' the fact that the original feeling remains unfinished. Just as he did in infancy, he concludes: 'Though I'm terrified, I still won't get my needs met, because I'm unlovable anyway. Therefore there's no point in my showing I'm terrified. In fact, I won't even let myself feel how terrified I am.'

This interplay of script beliefs and repressed feelings makes up the *feedback loop* shown by the dotted arrows in Figure 3.1. The entire process takes place intrapsychically. It remains outside the person's conscious awareness.

This is a closed system, in that the person is not making his script beliefs available for updating against here-and-now reality. Each time he replays his script beliefs, the man in our example achieves his infant objective of 'explaining away' his unmet needs. But in so doing, he blanks out other possible explanations of the situation that are more appropriate to his situation here-and-now. For instance, the woman concerned may not really have been rejecting him. Even if she were, that would still not imply that he is inherently unlovable. Most basic of all, he is blanking out the here-and-now reality that he *can* survive as a grown-up even if he happens to be rejected by an important woman.

Rackety Displays

When the person is engaged in this intrapsychic process, he manifests it in various ways that Erskine and Zalcman (1979) call *rackety displays*. These are listed in the central column of the Racket System diagram (Figure 3.1). They may include *observable behaviours, reported internal experiences* and *scripty fantasies*. All of these reflect strategies that the infant decided to adopt as a means of getting needs met when the expression of his original feeling had failed to do so. When in script as an adult, the person replays these old patterns.

Continuing our example: failing to get mother's attention by escalating terror, the infant may eventually discover she does respond to tantrums. Thus he learns to overlay his original feeling of terror with a substitute feeling of anger. He decides that expressing anger is his best means of manipulating others into meeting his needs.

Admittedly, when mother does respond to him now, she herself is angry and resentful. Her response may be to shout at the baby, even to shake or strike him. But at least she is giving him some attention, and this is far better than the dreadful alternative of being abandoned. Over time the child decides: 'If I'm to get any attention at all, it has to be negative attention. And the way I can arrange to get it is to throw tantrums until the important other person gets angry enough to give me the attention I need.'

When in script as an adult, the person re-enacts childhood strategies like these, together with their accompanying emotions. So long as the script beliefs remain unconfronted, these behaviours and feelings will be replayed over and over again as the person attempts to deal with the unfinished needs of childhood.

Sometimes rackety displays represent a defence against a script belief, rather than an expression of that belief. Consider again the person who decided in infancy 'I'm unlovable'. As an adult he might unknowingly defend against this belief by repetitively seeking sexual conquests in 'Don Juan' style.

As well as showing the overt behaviours included in rackety displays, the person may experience internal sensations such as tension or muscle pain, or somatic disturbances like blushing or indigestion.

Scripty fantasies

The person may also engage in fantasies that serve to further the script beliefs. Zalcman (1986) calls these *scripty fantasies*.

Continuing our example: this person in adulthood might have fantasies that people talk about him behind his back, discussing with each other all the things that are 'wrong with him'. Such fantasies often centre round 'the worst that could happen'. However, they may also sometimes portray a grandiose version of 'the best that could happen'. For instance, the same person may have an internal picture of the ideal woman who will give him unending love and attention. Both 'best' and 'worst' are equally unrealistic views of adult reality.

Reinforcing Memories

Each time the adult person in script re-runs a childhood strategy, it is likely to bring results similar to those it brought in childhood. Along with these will go the same emotions the person felt as a child. Thus each time the process is repeated, the person can say to himself outside of awareness: 'Yes, the world *is* like I thought it was.'

The person typically builds up a store of memories of these outcomes. When in script, she consults these memories. They provide 'evidence' in support of the script beliefs, and so serve to strengthen those beliefs. The right-hand column of the Racket System lists these *reinforcing memories*. By this repeating process of reinforcement, another closed feedback loop is formed on the Racket System. It is shown by the solid arrow in Figure 3.1.

Each reinforcing memory carries its own emotional charge. As the person stores away each memory, he also stores the emotion that went with it. Later, replaying the memory, he can also re-experience the stored emotion. Berne (1964b) used the wry phrase *trading stamps* to describe these stored-up feelings. It refers to the way in which some supermarkets used to give out coloured stamps to customers along with their purchases. When the customer collected enough stamps, he could trade them in for a 'free gift'. In the same way, the person in script may stack up emotional trading stamps. Eventually he may trade them in for a script payoff such as a headache, a quarrel, a lawsuit or a suicide.*

For everyone, there will in reality be many occasions when the outcome of behaviour does *not* support the script beliefs. However, when in script the person will typically blank these occasions out of his recollection. Reinforcing memories may include memories of fantasized events as well as actual events.

At this point in the chapter, we have completed an outline of how personal problems originate and how people maintain problems in adult life. Next comes the question: what can you do to help people resolve their problems?

The Task of the Counsellor

The converse of *script* is *autonomy*. When a person is acting auto-nomously, she meets here-and-now problems in ways that use her full resources as an adult. She responds to the present *in* the present, instead of repeating self-limiting strategies from her own past.

Thus your task as counsellor can be summarized in four words:

CONFRONT SCRIPT – INVITE AUTONOMY.

Whatever detailed therapeutic techniques you choose to use, this remains the basic purpose of intervention.

Key Ideas 3.4

AIMS OF INTERVENTION

1 An *effective intervention* is one that confronts the script and invites the client into autonomy.
2 A *harmful intervention* is one that invites the client to reinforce the script.
3 An *ineffectual intervention* is one that is irrelevant to the client's movement into or out of script.

---

*The critical reviewer for this 2007 edition pointed out to me that although 'trading stamps' have been consigned to history, many stores now have 'loyalty cards' that perform exactly the same function. Times, he says, have not really changed that much after all. True as that is, TA has stayed with Berne's original theory term 'trading stamp'.

I speak here of *inviting* autonomy or *inviting* reinforcement of script. This is to underline TA's philosophical stance that you cannot 'make' someone change, either for better or for worse. In the end it will be the client who decides to change or not change. Your skill is consistently to present him with the options he has available in his grown-up reality. In so doing, you confront his belief that he is still limited to the resources he had as a young child.

The meaning of confrontation

In TA usage, *confrontation* does not imply the use of aggressive or harsh interventions. It simply means any move you make that invites your client to test his script beliefs against here-and-now reality.

Stroking for Change

The converse of *confrontation* is *stroking*. To stroke, in this context, means to offer some kind of recognition or reward (see this chapter, in the section above on *Strokes and Stroke-seeking*). In the technical shorthand of TA, we can say that:

- An effective intervention *confronts script* and *strokes autonomy*.
- A harmful intervention is one that *strokes the script*.

From the discussion earlier in this chapter, you know that stroking is a powerful means of inviting the person to repeat whatever behaviour or feeling is being stroked. Thus whenever your client makes a move out of script and into autonomy, you can help her consolidate that move by stepping in to offer a stroke (Goulding and Goulding, 1979: 94).

Equally important is that you do *not* stroke script beliefs or their accompanying behaviours or feelings. Obviously you would not deliberately praise a person in a counselling session for destructive or painful behaviours. Recall, though, that the person in script is eager to see the world as 'confirming' her script beliefs. Therefore she will sometimes issue subtle invitations for you to join her in those beliefs. She may do this verbally or non-verbally, and will not be aware she is doing so. For example, she may:

- say things that belittle herself, you or others, and expect you to agree
- laugh when speaking of something painful
- say she wants something, but not ask you for it

- act helpless and hope you will solve her problems for her
- ventilate feelings in apparent 'catharsis' but not change anything
- say something in words and signal something different in her behaviour.

Your skill is to detect all these invitations and decline each one. In Chapter 9, I shall describe ways in which you can do this.

Interventions on the Racket System

In terms of the Racket System, the aim of intervention is to help your client break out of the old feedback loops and replace them with new options.

Note that there is a difference between *interrupting* the flow of the Racket System and *breaking free* from it permanently (Zalcman, 1986; Erskine and Moursund, 1988). To escape the Racket System permanently, the person must do two things:

- Update his script beliefs.
- Resolve the script feelings that accompany these beliefs.

As the person changes in these ways, he can go on to achieve permanent changes in the behaviours, thoughts, feelings and bodily patterns that made up the rest of the system. It is as though the script beliefs and feelings were the 'powerhouse' for the entire Racket System.

By contrast, what happens if the person simply makes an initial change at one of the other points in the system, but does not attend to script beliefs or feelings? For example, suppose someone who has habitually withdrawn from social contact makes up his mind to attend a social club and open conversation with at least one person he meets there. This behaviour marks a move out of one of his rackety displays. It is a genuine change, since it interrupts the predictable flow of the Racket System.

But so long as the person's script beliefs and feelings remain unchanged, it is likely that he may soon find some other way of 'confirming' the script beliefs. In our example, this person might walk into the social club and choose to speak to someone who had her own scripty reasons to be distant or down-putting to him. Experiencing her rejection, he might say to himself outside of awareness: 'Ah well, I was right after all. It isn't safe for me to relate to people.'

Thus as you use the Racket System as a guide to intervention, your main task will be to help your client update her script beliefs and resolve the accompanying script feelings.

This said, there are good reasons for paying attention also to all the other parts of the system. The client's presenting problem will often lie in her rackety displays. You may choose to make an *initial* intervention by asking your client to interrupt the system at any point. You can do this by asking her to change her thinking, her feelings, her behaviour, or the way she uses her body (Erskine and Moursund, 1988). This initial change can often provide you and the client with a 'key' into the more fundamental change of script beliefs and feelings.*

Again, when someone has achieved a change in a script belief, he will usually need to follow this up with a period of behavioural practice if he is to integrate the new patterns fully into his life. I return to this point in Chapter 10.

Throughout Part II of this book I shall use the Racket System as an organizing scheme for both assessment and intervention.

There is one more element of TA's explanatory framework to look at in the next and final chapter of Part I. It is the ego-state model, the account of personality that is at the foundation of TA theory and practice.

---

* In Chapter 11, where we deal with 'Ending Counselling', you will see that Eric Berne (1961, 1972) describes the process of 'cure' as entailing four successive stages. His first two stages, *social control* and *symptomatic relief*, correspond closely to what we are here calling 'interrupting the Racket System'. When the person 'breaks free from the Racket System', she is achieving Berne's fourth suggested stage of cure, namely *script cure*.

4

SEPARATING PAST FROM PRESENT

Theory of Ego-states
Identifying Ego-states

A recurring theme in Chapter 3 was the distinction between the past and the present. At times the person will behave, think and feel in ways that are direct responses to what is going on here and now. At other times his behaviours, thoughts and feelings are responses to situations from his own past.

In this chapter I present a model that focuses on this distinction between past and present. It is known as the *ego-state model* (Berne, 1961, 1966; Clarkson, 1992: 40–54; Erskine and Moursund, 1988; Sills and Hargaden, 2003; Stewart, 1992: 22–31; Stewart and Joines, 1987: 11–55).

The basic idea of the ego-state model is straightforward. It is that you can reliably judge *by observation* whether someone is responding to present time or replaying patterns from the past.

In the first part of this chapter I outline the theory of ego-states. The second section describes how you can identify ego-states in practice. It includes an extended self-supervision sequence that you can use to help sharpen your skill in ego-state diagnosis.

I have included this chapter in Part I's discussion of 'The TA Framework' rather than in the description of the treatment sequence in Part II. This is because the ego-state model is a fundamental part of TA theory. Likewise, the skill of identifying ego-states is basic to all TA practice, whatever the field to which you may apply it.

THE EGO-STATE MODEL

1   At certain times the person will be behaving, thinking and feeling in ways that replay his own childhood. At such times he is said to be in a *Child ego-state.*
2   At other moments the person may behave, think and feel in ways he has copied in childhood from his parents or parent-figures. He is then said to be in a *Parent ego-state.*
3   When the person's behaviour, thoughts and feelings are neither replayed from his childhood nor borrowed from parental figures, but instead are direct responses to the here-and-now, he is said to be in an *Adult ego-state.*

Theory of Ego-states

In everyday TA usage, we frequently say simply that the person is 'in Child', 'in Parent' or 'in Adult'. When the words Parent, Adult and Child are used to designate ego-states, they are spelt with an initial capital. The same words beginning with small letters signal an actual parent, adult or child.

Definition of ego-states

Thus the ego-state model focuses on three ways that people have of expressing personality. Each way is defined by a distinctive and *observable* set of behaviours. The model next asserts that each set of behaviours will be *consistently* accompanied by a set of thoughts and feelings which typify that ego-state. Though the thoughts and feelings are not directly observable, they can be checked by questioning the person.

This gives the definition of an ego-state: 'a consistent pattern of feeling and experience directly related to a corresponding consistent pattern of behaviour' (Berne, 1966: 364).

There is no suggestion that ego-states occupy any particular locations in the brain or the body. Indeed, ego-states are not concrete entities of any kind. They are simply *names*. The terms Parent, Adult and Child are three labels which we use to designate these three distinct sets of behaviours, thoughts and feelings.

Ego-states and the time dimension

The time dimension is crucial to Berne's original concept of the ego-state model. When the person is in Child, she is replaying behaviours, thoughts and feelings *from her own past*, that is, her childhood. Berne underlined this by referring to the Child as an *archaic* ego-state.

In Parent, the person is using ways of behaving, thinking and feeling that she uncritically copied *in the past* from her parents and parent-figures. To express this, Berne called the Parent a *borrowed* ego-state.

Only in Adult is the person acting, thinking and feeling in ways that are direct responses to the *present*.

How is the Ego-state Model Useful?

The practical uses of the ego-state model in counselling become clear when we summarize what we know of it so far:

* The model asserts that the three types of ego-state can be reliably distinguished one from the other by observation and questioning.
* Thus you are able to judge from moment to moment whether the person is:

  – replaying his own childhood (Child)
  – replaying material borrowed from his parents or parent-figures (Parent)
  – responding directly to the here-and-now (Adult).

* By learning to recognize your own ego-state patterns, you become able to monitor your own responses to the client under these same three headings.
* This knowledge in turn helps you and your client *choose* which of these responses you want to make.

Another practical reason for learning about the ego-state model is that it forms the foundation for most other areas of TA theory.

Identifying Ego-states

The skill of recognizing ego-state shifts is basic to TA practice. Eric Berne (1961: 66–9) listed four modes of ego-state diagnosis:

* behavioural
* social
* historical
* phenomenological.

He stressed that wherever possible all four of these should be used, preferably in the order given above.

Behavioural Diagnosis

As its name implies, this means the diagnosis of ego-states by observation of behavioural clues. Each ego-state will be signalled by a consistent combination of:

* words
* tones
* gestures
* postures
* facial expressions.

There will also be finer physiological clues such as changes in breathing or heart rate.

Behavioural clues: standard or unique?

When a person is in Child, she is not just behaving as 'children generally' behave. She is behaving as *she* used to behave in her own unique childhood. In Parent, she is using behaviours she has borrowed from *her own* unique parents, not just behaviours typical of 'parents in general'.

It follows that each person will have her own unique set of behavioural clues for each ego-state. For instance, my set of clues for Parent will mirror the behaviours of my own parents, and perhaps of other parent-figures of mine like grandparents and schoolteachers. They will be different from the behavioural clues you show when you are in Parent, because your parent-figures were different from mine.

The empirical work done on ego-state identification, particularly by Steere (1982), has confirmed that the detailed behavioural clues for each ego-state are unique to the individual, not uniform as between individuals.

Behavioural diagnosis in practice

But given that behavioural clues to ego-states are different from one individual to the next, how is behavioural diagnosis possible?

The answer is that though the fine detail of ego-state behaviours does differ as between individuals, there are certain common behavioural signals that frequently indicate a particular ego-state. The reason for this is not hard to find. Though my parents and yours were different people, there are certain behaviours that *parents in general* do typically exhibit when they are controlling or caring for their children. And though we were different children, we had in common a repertoire of behaviours often shown by *children in general* when adapting to or rebelling against parental directives, or when acting in a spontaneous fashion.

You can therefore make a useful start in behavioural diagnosis if you watch for such generally 'parent-like' or 'child-like' behaviours. To be fully effective in using the ego-state model, however, you need to stay aware that judgements founded on these general clues are only a starting point.

To improve the reliability of your behavioural diagnosis, you need to compile a detailed list of the unique ego-state behaviours shown by each person. This requires that you observe that person over time. It also requires that you continually cross-relate your behavioural observations from moment to moment with the person's reports of feelings, thoughts and beliefs. Without such reports, you have no way of checking whether your intuitions about the ego-state behaviours shown by that individual are accurate or not.

It is by this continued process of cross-checking that you will develop the skill of behavioural diagnosis. Berne commended the use of *intuitive* judgement, and this surprisingly often does give an accurate reading of a person's ego-state. However, Berne had had the benefit of years of experience in working with clients within the framework of the ego-state model. He had continually had the opportunity to cross-check his intuitive behavioural diagnoses with the clients' reports of thoughts, beliefs and feelings. Well aware of the importance of this feedback, he urged that behavioural diagnosis wherever possible should be correlated with the other three modes of diagnosis: social, historical and phenomenological.

Social Diagnosis

In social diagnosis, you judge a person's ego-state by noting the ego-state responses he gets from others. This is based on the observation that if a person manifests a particular ego-state he will reliably invite a complementary ego-state in the other person. If he shows Child, the chances are good that he will get a response from Parent. If he exhibits his own Parent ego-state he will probably invite Child in response. If he comes from Adult, the likelihood is that he will get a response back from Adult.

You may be asking yourself: 'But isn't social diagnosis just a matter of applying behavioural diagnosis to two people rather than one? So why list it as a separate class of diagnosis?' In my experience, the main practical usefulness of social diagnosis is to help you track ego-state exchanges between your client and *yourself*. If, for example, you realize that you are feeling or behaving in a Parental manner toward your client – if, for example, you feel like sorting them out or telling them off – social diagnosis would lead you to hypothesize that they were coming on to you from a Child ego-state. For this diagnostic method to be effective, of course, you need to have developed the skill of being aware of your own ego-state shifts. An excellent way of enhancing this skill is to take tapes of your sessions to supervision, and focus with your supervisor on the ego-state shifts shown both by your client and by yourself.

If you are familiar with the language of psychodynamic counselling, you will realize that this use of social diagnosis implies being aware of your *countertransference* on the client. In current psychodynamic usage, we might define 'countertransference' in broad terms as 'the sum total of feelings, thoughts and responses that you bring forward from your own past experience and "put in front of" another person whom you are relating to in the present'. We can express the same idea in TA language by saying that we often 'put faces on' other people. These 'faces' are the faces of people from our own past. Sometimes we may 'put a Parent face' on the other, in which case we ourselves are likely to relate to them from Child; or we may 'put a Child face' on the other person and seek to relate to them as if we were their Parent.*

In traditional psychoanalytic language, this process has been called 'transference' when it is the client who is 'putting a face on' the counsellor, and 'countertransference' when the counsellor 'puts a face on' the client. In present-day usage, it is widely agreed that the entire process is in fact two-way and mutual: client and counsellor may well each 'put a face on' the other.

Thus, returning to our example of social diagnosis: if you feel Parental toward your client, that will be because at that moment you are 'putting a Child face' on him. In social diagnosis, the assumption is that your client

---

*This practical textbook is not the place to embark on a detailed discussion of the various meanings that different writers have attached to the terms 'transference' and 'countertransference', either in TA or in psychotherapy and counselling generally. I hope, therefore, that my working description of 'countertransference' here will suffice for practical application. In any case, Berne's original theory of ego-states, transactions and script is *already* a theory of transference and countertransference, and was always meant to be so (cf. Erskine, 1991; Stewart, 1992: 36–9). For more detailed discussions of the role of transference and countertransference in TA, see Clarkson, 1992: 148–74; Cornell and Hargaden, 2005.

has *invited* you to do that, by actually communicating with you from his own Child ego-state (and 'putting a Parent face' on you). His 'invitation', of course, will be outside of his conscious awareness. Your task as counsellor is to monitor your own response, and as far as possible bring it *into* your conscious awareness. This means developing and using the skill of recognizing your own shifts in ego-state.

You will see from this that social diagnosis is potentially a more complex matter than it appears to be from the simple description we started with. Once again, careful use of supervision is the key to developing your Adult awareness of the 'faces' you may be putting on your clients, and they on you.

Historical Diagnosis

In historical diagnosis you check behavioural ego-state clues by asking the person questions about his childhood and about the people who figured in it. This relies on the fact that a Child ego-state designates a replay of material from the person's own childhood, while Parent is borrowed from parental figures who had specific identities. Thus if you see the person showing behaviours that seem to fit with your intuitive notion of Child, you might make a historical check by asking:

'Does the way you're behaving now remind you of anything in your childhood?'

You might follow up with questions like:

'What are you saying to yourself in your head as you behave this way?'
'Was that something you said to yourself as a child?'
'What age were you at the time?'

If you observe the person showing behaviours that look like Parent, your question might be:

'Hold that position for a second. Did either of your parents take up that body position when you were young?'

For historical diagnosis of Adult, we rely on the definition of the Adult ego-state 'by difference'. If a person is showing behaviours that intuitively seem Adult, we can make historical checks to discover whether she is replaying childhood patterns or copying parent-figures. If not, our behavioural diagnosis of Adult is supported.

Phenomenological Diagnosis

At times, the person may not merely remember past events, but re-experience them as though they were happening in the present. When this takes place, you have the material for a phenomenological diagnosis. For instance, a client during a counselling session, talking about a childhood loss, may get in contact with the sadness she felt at that time and burst out crying. She not only shows behavioural clues to Child, but also re-experiences the entire childhood scene and the emotions that went with it.

Self-supervision 4.1

IDENTIFYING EGO-STATES

If you wish to follow the stages of TA treatment with one of your clients, select that client now. You may choose that this should be someone you are already seeing. Alternatively, you may begin at the beginning with a new client.

(a) Initial identification of behavioural clues

Make an initial judgement of your client's behavioural ego-state clues. You can do this during a face-to-face session. Even better, you can make a video or audiotape recording, if your institutional setting allows. Tell the client beforehand that you are doing this. After the session, play the recording through many times and pick out ego-state clues.

   At this early stage, simply rely upon your intuition to judge whether your client is replaying her own childhood (Child), reproducing material she copied from parental figures (Parent) or responding as her present grown-up self (Adult).

   Ego-state clues can change from second to second. This means that to develop the skill of detecting behavioural clues to ego-state shifts, you need to become used to assessing your client's behavioural signals as they are shown in these brief time-periods. Depending upon the mode of counselling in which you have been trained, this may mean that you have to alter your mental set about the way you observe clients.

(b) Check for ego-state consistency

Return to the instances of Child ego-state behaviours that you identified in your client. Check whether she exhibits these behaviours *as a consistent*

(Continued)

set. You can do this by further observation of the client, or by re-checking your tape of a past session. Here again, be ready to alter your timescale if necessary so that you stay aware of the client's behavioural clues as they change from one second to the next.

Consider any thoughts and feelings which the client reports while performing the behaviours that you have initially identified as Child. Does the client consistently report these feelings together with these thoughts? Are these reports in accord with the definition of Child as a replay of material from the client's own childhood?

Do these reported thoughts and emotions consistently accompany the behaviours which you identified as Child?

Carry out the same steps for the instances of Parent and of Adult behaviours which you initially identified in your client.

(c)   Extending behavioural diagnosis

Return to the sets of behavioural clues you have listed so far as indicating Child, Parent and Adult ego-states for this client. Extend this now by listing any further behavioural clues which you identify as being associated with each of her ego-states. Consider words, tones, gestures, postures and facial expressions. You may also list other physiological clues if you are aware of them, for example, heart rate, breathing, muscular tensions.

Bear in mind that you are looking for signals that you observe occurring *consistently* together. You may also check by report on the client's thoughts and feelings as these further behaviours are shown.

(d)   Social diagnosis

Review the instances you listed at step *(a)* of occasions when you judged your client to be in Child, in Parent and in Adult. Consider the ego-state responses you showed to her at these times. When she was in Child, did you respond in Parent? At times when she was in Parent, did you have an impulse to respond from Child? When she came from Adult, were you also in an Adult ego-state? On what behavioural and experiential clues of your own do you base these judgements?

(e)   Historical and phenomenological diagnosis

Using questioning, you may now add historical and phenomenological diagnosis as further checks on ego-state identification. For example, at

(Continued)

(Continued)

moments when you judge that your client may be 'replaying her childhood', you can enquire whether she is recalling childhood memories (historical) or re-experiencing some childhood scene (phenomenological). Which time or times in her childhood has she been replaying? What age was she on each occasion? Similarly for Parent: which parent or parent-figure, by name, was she copying? Check whether on the occasions on which you identified the client as being in Adult, she was neither replaying her childhood nor reproducing parental behaviours, thoughts or feelings.

Now, at the close of Part I, you have met the two concepts that are the defining features of TA: ego-states and the life-script. These two ideas are basic to TA theory, hence to everything you will do in TA practice.

In Part II we go on to look at that practice in detail. What steps do you follow as you apply transactional analysis in counselling?

Part II

THE PROCESS OF COUNSELLING WITH TA

5

TAKING THE FIRST STEPS

First Contact and Intake
Criteria for Referral
The Business Contract

As a practising counsellor, you will already have your own intake procedure. You will also have criteria that you use when deciding whether to work with a person or refer him to another professional. In this chapter, I review the intake and referral procedures typical of TA practice, and outline the business contracts. As an illustration, I describe intake with my client 'John'. You may find some of these ideas useful to incorporate into your own work.

First Contact and Intake

When you and your client first make contact, you have no contract to work together. Yet in TA practice, the concept of *contractual method* defines your objectives even at this initial stage. If two parties are considering entering into a contract, their first step must be to get to know relevant facts about each other. What does each party want from the contractual relationship, and what is each able and willing to give to it? You may not be able to answer these questions in complete detail at this stage, but they need to be answered fully enough to allow each party to decide whether to go ahead with the contract.

Thus one of your purposes at first contact and during intake is to get an initial picture of the other person in enough detail to allow you to decide if you will enter into a counselling contract with him. Equally important is that you give him whatever information about you he needs to make the same decision. Cornell (1986) suggests opening the way for this by asking your potential client 'What do you need to know about me?'

At the same time, you need to bear in mind that you and your client have not yet made a contract. Neither of you has said clearly what you want from the other, nor agreed what you are willing to give in return. Therefore it is not appropriate for you to volunteer counselling interventions to the other person at this stage. Neither is it protective of yourself to accept any overt or covert invitations the other person may issue to begin work on personal change before the contract has been agreed.

First Contact

My own practice at first contact is to keep any initial telephone conversation as short as possible. Instead I invite the person to make an appointment for a half-hour interview at a time agreed between us. The purpose of this interview is for the person and myself to discover the information we need to know about each other to make the decision whether to work together. As part of this information, I specify the nature of confidentiality and the circumstances in which I would break it.

I do not charge for this initial interview. If by the end of it we have tentatively decided to begin a counselling relationship, I tell the client that the next step will be to complete a formal intake. I make clear that if he agrees to this I shall begin charging him for my time, even if it emerges on completing the intake that we shall not after all be working together. Often, the intake interview runs on directly from the end of the initial interview.

Some other transactional analysts prefer to have a longer initial telephone conversation, using it in the same way as I use the initial interview (see for example, Cornell, 1986).

John: First Contact and Initial Interview

As usual in my practice, my first contact with John was when he telephoned me. He had heard of me via a friend-of-a-friend with whom I had worked some time earlier. During our conversation I asked him to describe briefly the problem he wanted to resolve. He replied in general terms: he had 'a problem in relating to his girlfriend'.

I gave him a brief description of the kind of work I do, and stated my charges. I told him that if he wanted to pursue the idea of working with me, I would ask him to fix an initial half-hour appointment. I made it clear that I would not charge for this initial session. I explained that its sole purpose would be for John and myself to exchange further information and decide mutually whether we would begin working together. He said he wanted to do this, and we fixed a time for our initial discussion.

At this opening interview I listened to John's presenting problem. I made no interventions except to ask for more information when I wanted it.

John told me that he was in a live-in relationship with his girl-friend Helen. He felt he loved her and wanted their relationship to be permanent, though neither of them was considering getting married in the immediate future. Yet he had frequently been getting into quarrels with Helen, and these had been growing more severe as time went on. During one of these rows in the past week, he had hit her.

I interrupted to ask: 'Hit her with what?'

John replied: 'With my hand.'

He had slapped Helen in a way that caused her no permanent physical damage. However, she had told John she had 'just about had enough', and was threatening to leave him.

John recognized uncomfortably that he had played out a similar pattern with two earlier girlfriends, both of whom had eventually left him. He wanted to avoid doing the same again. Yet he felt he did not know how to control his temper, and was scared he might end up losing Helen in the same way as he had lost his past girlfriends.

As I listened to John, I was checking for any features in his presentation that even at this stage might indicate a need to refer him to another professional. However, I noted nothing that pointed immediately to possible psychosis or medical problems. So far, the way seemed clear for us to work together. I therefore went on to tell John some essential things about what that work would involve.

Confidentiality

I told John that if he decided to come to me for counselling, I would tape-record all our sessions. (This is normal TA practice. It reflects the importance that transactional analysts attach to the detailed supervision and self-supervision of taped work.) I assured John that the tapes, and any other verbal or written information to do with our work together, would remain confidential between us. I also made clear that I reserved the following two exceptions:

* I might use some of the information in consultations with my supervisor. If I did so, I would identify John only by his first name.
* If John gave me any information that seemed to me to indicate an immediate threat to his life or health, or anybody else's, I reserved the right to report that information to his doctor, to emergency medical services, or to the police. I made it clear that I would only use this facility as a last resort, if I judged there was no other practical way to avoid these outcomes. (John and Helen had no children, and there was no indication that any child could be affected by the outcome of the case. Had a child been potentially involved, I would also have told John that I reserved the right to break confidentiality to the appropriate authorities if I had any concerns over child abuse.)

I asked John if I had his agreement to these exceptions. He gave it. If he had refused permission to any part of this, I would have ended the interview, making clear to him why I was doing so.

As it was, John and I now went on to complete an intake questionnaire.

The Intake Questionnaire

Like most transactional analysts, I use a relatively brief intake interview. It has three main purposes:

* To identify the client.
* To get a more detailed view of the presenting problem.
* To reveal any features that might indicate a need for referral.

The following are the questions I use in my intake interview. Most TA practitioners use a similar sequence. The questions are listed in italic type. Comments on the purpose of particular questions follow in roman type.

1   *Name, address, telephone number?*
2   *Age and date of birth?*
3   *Present occupation?*

4 *Marital status? With whom are you living at present?* For this and the
   previous question, you may follow up by asking the person how he
   feels about his job and his living situation.
5 *Children? If so, age and sex of each?*
6 *Address and telephone number of general practitioner?*
7 *Any past or present physical complaints? If so, what treatment are you
   receiving (have you received) for these?* This may alert you to physical
   problems that will restrict the kinds of work you can do with this person. For instance, if she has chronic back pain it may not be advisable
   to invite her into physical rage release. Then there is a whole range of
   somatic complaints that may sometimes be related to script issues.
   These include muscular tension, aches and pains, digestive upsets,
   high blood pressure and so on. If the person reports any such complaint, whether it is the presenting problem or not, it is necessary to
   follow up by asking whether she is already receiving medical treatment for it. I return to this topic under 'referral criteria' below.
8 *Have you ever had any serious accidents?* Most transactional analysts
   assume that any accident was deliberate unless there is clear evidence
   to the contrary. 'Deliberate' here does not mean that the person was
   necessarily aware of setting up the accident. A 'yes' answer to this
   question will flag up for you the necessity to explore the issue of self-
   harm, whether or not the person raises it overtly.
9 *Any past or present psychiatric complaints? If so, what treatment are
   you receiving (have you received) for these?* The answer here may give
   immediate grounds for referral (see below).
10 *Is there anyone in your immediate family who is suffering (has suffered)
   from a psychiatric complaint?* This can give useful clues to some
   features of the life-script (see Chapter 6).
11 *Are you under any form of medication at this time?* The answer gives a
   double-check on the possible need for referral. It also gives more information on the kinds of work you can do with the person. If he is taking
   minor tranquillizers or anti-depressants, you know these drugs will be
   altering his perception of the problem he has brought to counselling.
   You and the person may sooner or later want to consider his reducing
   or ceasing these medications. Again, this means you must refer the person for the advice of his GP or psychiatrist. There are some medications
   that are not given primarily for psychiatric complaints but which may be
   relevant to your treatment plan, for example, beta-blockers.
12 *How much alcohol do you drink per week? And how is this total
   divided up between different days of the week?* The second part of the

question checks whether the client, though reporting a relatively small overall intake of alcohol, may indulge in 'binge drinking'.

13   *How much tea, coffee or cola do you drink per day?* This is of interest when the presenting problem includes anxiety, insomnia, tremor or palpitations.

14   *Do you smoke?* Transactional analysts have varying opinions on whether smoking is always a covert means of self-harm. I believe it is, and this is probably the majority view in current TA. Thus stopping smoking becomes a high priority in the treatment plan, whether or not the person brings it as the presenting problem.

15   *Do you take (have you ever taken) non-prescribed drugs?* If the person is currently a substance-abuser, you have grounds for immediate referral. This also applies to excessive drinking revealed by the answer to question 12. Abuse of drugs or alcohol does not necessarily mean that you cannot work with the person. It does mean that any work needs to be undertaken with medical consent and specialized support.

16   *Have you ever been in trouble with the police, other than for minor traffic offences?* This may give a clue to a character-disorder diagnosis. Alternatively, the person who reports trouble with the law may have been acting out self-harm issues.

17   *How much do you know about TA?* If the answer is 'nothing', you may want to prescribe reading or suggest the person attends a basic course on TA. Opinions on this vary in current TA circles. Some practitioners like to use TA language and draw up TA models during discussions with their clients. Others prefer to 'think TA' but avoid using TA terms when speaking with the client.

The presenting problem

It is likely that you will have heard the person's presenting problem before you begin the formal intake, as was the case in my interview with John. Now you may find it useful to summarize the problem on your intake record. You may offer your summarized version to the person and ask him whether you have understood the problem correctly.

John: Intake Summary

John confirmed that he was not suffering from any medical complaint, and was not taking any kind of medication at the time of intake. He had had no life-threatening accidents. However, he had had a brief period of out-patient treatment about five years before coming to me. The problem then, as now, was that he had been having trouble in relating to a woman. He said he had been diagnosed as 'suffering from stress' and had been prescribed tranquillizers, which he had taken for a few weeks and then discontinued. John volunteered the information that on this earlier occasion also he had struck his girlfriend with his fist. She had responded by ending their relationship.

There was no history of mental disorder in John's immediate family. He reported smoking about five cigarettes per day. Until the fracas with Helen, he had regularly been drinking about four pints of beer per night. It was after a drinking session that he had struck her. I made a mental note that this level of drinking was well above the recommended guidelines for alcohol intake. However, John reported that since that occasion he had cut his drinking to about one pint per night. His general health was intact. I therefore decided on balance that I did not need to refer him for specialized help in the area of alcohol abuse.

Self-supervision 5.1

INTAKE

If your chosen client is one whom you have already been seeing for some time, review the questions in the intake questionnaire above, and supply the answers from what you already know of the client. You may then wish to fill in the remainder of the information at your next session with this client.

If you are beginning with a new client, follow the procedure described above for first contact and intake. Review the answers you note for the questions in the intake interview and check what they reveal to you about the client.

With the intake complete, you can now move to a decision whether to work with the person or refer him to someone else. In the coming section of the chapter, I describe the considerations that are relevant to this decision.

Criteria for Referral

How can you judge whether to work with a person or refer him to some-one else? The TA concept of the 'three Ps' (see Chapter 1) gives you one way of answering this question. You should refer the person if you cannot offer enough *permission*, *protection* or *potency*. Of the three, protection is the most important.

Protection

The question here is: 'If I go ahead and work with this person, what chance is there that the person, I or anyone else is going to come to harm?' You can never answer this question with complete certainty. However, there are some circumstances in which referral is clearly indicated:

- *Medical referral*: where there is any significant possibility that the person is suffering from a physical disorder, you must refer her to a medical practitioner. (It is increasingly common practice for counsel-lors to recommend their clients to have a full medical check-up, even when no physical disorder is reported, to rule out any organic basis for mood changes or behavioural difficulties).
- *Psychiatric referral*: if you detect any sign of a possible psychotic diagnosis, you must refer the person for a psychiatric opinion.
- *Substance-abusers*: if the potential client abuses alcohol or other sub-stances, you would proceed as described for medical or psychiatric referral, unless you are already working in a setting with the necessary facilities for support.
- *Conflict of interest*: to avoid the possibility of exploitation, you should not work with anyone with whom you already have a close relation-ship, whether personal, sexual or financial.

The client on medication

When a client is taking minor tranquillizers or anti-depressants pre-scribed by her doctor, you and she may well agree at some point in your work that it would be a good idea for her to come off these drugs. However, you cannot suggest that she do so unless you have at least the tacit consent of her GP. My usual procedure in these cases is to write to the doctor informing him that the person has told me she is taking the drugs concerned. I say that if his patient comes into counselling with me, the time may come when she will be ready to reduce and eventually cease to use these medications. I tell the GP that if I do not hear from him to the contrary, I shall take it that he agrees to my using my judgement in recommending to his patient that she proceeds in this way.

Referral in emergencies

Having an emergency during a session is on a par with your house catching on fire. You hope and expect it will never happen, and to most people it never does. However, you need to be ready to deal with it if it does happen.

In the last resort in any emergency, you may have to call a doctor, an ambulance or the police. You must therefore have a telephone within a few seconds' reach at all times when you are conducting sessions. Emergency telephone numbers need to be available beside it. These include the telephone number of your client's GP, which you noted during the intake interview.

What if you have reason to believe your client intends imminent suicide or self-harm? In Chapter 7, I describe the TA procedure that is usually used to guard against this outcome. It entails the client stating a period of time during which she will not, in any circumstances, harm self or others. However, she may not be willing to make this statement for even the shortest period. In that emergency, you need to stop the session and telephone her GP. If the doctor is not available, your next step is to call an ambulance. Until the client is safely in medical care, you must not leave her presence.

Other cases of medical or psychiatric emergency may possibly arise during a session. For instance, the client may suffer a heart attack or begin hallucinating. In these cases you would use your judgement in calling either the GP or an ambulance.

What if the client is threatening to harm others? Here again, the preferred option in TA practice is to ask the client to state a period during which he will not take any such action (see Chapter 7). Suppose, however, he refuses. At worst, he may leave the session saying he intends a physical attack on someone.

As a private practitioner, you have no responsibility for physically restraining violent clients. Indeed, any attempt at this might render you liable to prosecution. Your only action, therefore, is that of last resort: to call the police.

It may happen that a client telephones you from home or elsewhere threatening imminent suicide or violence. Your first response is to invite her to fix a session with you in the near future. You would ask her to agree firmly not to take any harmful action before that time. She may refuse. Your response then is to call either an ambulance or the police, whichever is appropriate to the threatened action, as soon as the client rings off. Therefore the first thing you need to do in your conversation with the client is to find out where she is calling from.

Permission

At the initial interview, you will have formed an idea of what permissions the person will need to take if she is to make the changes she wants. The question to ask yourself then is: 'How far have I taken these permissions myself?' You can only facilitate a client to achieve a goal to the same extent as you yourself have achieved it.

Suppose a person comes to you asking for help in resolving a problem, and you know that you still have the same problem. An example would be if the person's presenting problem was that he could not stop over-working, and you knew that you were also a compulsive worker. In a situation like this you have two choices: you may refer the person to another counsellor who does not have this problem, or you may go into counselling or therapy yourself to resolve your own difficulty. Your task then is to stay one step ahead of the client as you facilitate his changing on the same issue. If you choose this latter course, you need to tell the person what you intend doing before entering into a counselling contract.

Potency

The question to ask about potency is: 'Do I have the skills necessary to work with this person?' This is partly a matter of general skill and experience. A novice counsellor is unlikely to show the same potency as a case-hardened veteran, no matter who the client may be.

Partly also, potency may imply specialized skills needed for work with particular client-groups. Children, aged clients, substance-abusers and character-disordered clients are all groups whom you might decide to refer unless you have the specialized training needed to work with them. Another ground for referral might be if the person came to you with a problem which might benefit from work with a specialized counsellor, for example, bereavement or careers counselling.

John: Referral Criteria

From the evidence of the intake interview, there was no indication that I needed to refer John on medical or psychiatric grounds. There was no conflict of interest. In my private-practice setting, I could extend John sufficient protection, and I judged I had the potency to work with him successfully.

There were some questions in the area of permission. I recognized that some of John's unfinished childhood needs were the same as my own, and that he and I might therefore sometimes show similar maladaptive ways of dealing with the world under stress. As infants we had both decided that people were painfully unpredictable, and that it was therefore safer to be suspicious of others than to get close to them. The repetitive behaviour which John reported, that of testing relationships to destruction, had been part of my own adult life. However, I knew that in the course of my own personal change I had confronted that painful pattern. While I still engaged in it occasionally, I did so less often and less intensely than in the past. I decided therefore that I could model permission for John to change in the same way. If I contacted any still-unfinished business of my own around these old patterns of mistrust and rejection, I would need to resolve it in supervision or by re-entering counselling.

Self-supervision 5.2

REFERRAL CRITERIA

You may find it useful to note your answers to the following questions.

1. Which persons would you not work with?
2. What are your reasons for not working with these persons? How far can you relate each answer to the areas of protection, permission or potency?
3. What system do you have for referring each client-group with whom you would not work?

(Continued)

(Continued)

4 Review the classes of clients you *do* work with. Check that you can provide these clients with adequate protection, permission and potency.
5 Consider the possible emergencies mentioned in this chapter. What
procedures do you have ready to deal with these? Are you satisfied
they offer enough protection to you and your client?

Having checked and cleared referral criteria, I told John I was willing to
work with him. He said he wanted to go ahead. We thus went on to negotiate our *business contract*.

The Business Contract

The business contract is a mutual agreement about:

• Administrative details such as times, place and dates.
• Fees or other means of reward.
• Frequency and duration of sessions.
• Initial number of sessions.
• Possibly, purposes of specific sessions, for example, that early sessions
may be devoted to problem formulation, or that one particular session
(the sixth, say) may be for assessment or further contract-making.
• Advance arrangements for the termination of counselling, for exam-
ple, that the client will give at least two clear sessions' notice if she
wishes to terminate.

In making the business contract, you do not yet have the aim of reach-
ing detailed agreement about what or how the client wants to change in
counselling. That will be the task of the *treatment contract*, which forms a
later stage in the treatment sequence (see Chapter 8).

As regards the practical detail of frequency, duration and number of
sessions, TA has no distinctive procedure to offer. Like counsellors from
other disciplines, transactional analysts make their own decisions on these
matters on the basis of pragmatic rules-of-thumb. Weekly sessions are the
most usual; generally this is a long enough break to allow both parties
time to assimilate the work done in the previous session, while not being

so long that personal contact begins to be lost. The weekly session also has the practical advantage that it can be 'blocked into' the diaries of counsellor and client if they find this convenient. For one-to-one sessions, the traditional 'fifty-minute hour' is still the most usual. As a rule, this length of session gives counsellor and client sufficient time to settle into the work at hand, while not being so long that they risk running out of energy.

Once intake has been completed, most transactional analysts ask their clients to commit themselves to a minimum initial number of sessions. Again there is no standard number that all TA practitioners would agree on, but it typically varies between five and ten. The purpose of this initial commitment is to allow time for groundwork such as client assessment and problem formulation before the work of change begins. It is usual to specify that the last session of this initial number will be devoted to a mutual discussion of progress, and that a further number of sessions (or, alternatively, termination of counselling) can be agreed upon at that time.

Contract vs. Rules

The provisions of a contract are negotiable between you and your client. By contrast, *rules* are not open to negotiation. They are requirements you set for the potential client as prerequisites of your working together. For obvious reasons, you need to state your rules before finalizing the business contract.

Here are the conditions I state to every client. I make clear that it is open to the client to agree or not agree to any of these points, but that I shall only be willing to work with him if he does agree to all of them.

- I shall tape all or some sessions.
- Though sessions will be confidential, I require the right to break confidentiality in specific circumstances (spelled out as in an earlier section of this chapter).
- The client undertakes that during sessions she will not commit physical harm against herself or me, or cause damage to the room, fittings or furniture.
- The client agrees not to come to any session while under the influence of alcohol or non-prescribed drugs.

- If the client misses a session for any reason whatsoever, or is late for a session, I reserve the right to charge all or part of my fee for the time concerned.
- If the client wishes to terminate before the minimum number of sessions for which he and I have currently contracted, he must give notice of his intention to do so no later than the beginning of the session *before* the one that he now wishes to be his last session. If he does not do so, I reserve the right to charge all or part of my fee for the remaining sessions contracted.

The rationale for all these rules can be found in Crossman's principle of *protection* (recall Chapter 1). The rules serve as protection both for the client and for myself. Other transactional analysts may set rules that differ somewhat from mine, but my own practice is typical. For maximum clarity, I have a written copy of my rules that I give to each potential client for reference.

Whenever you set a rule, you must also have a *sanction*. You may choose to tell your potential client in advance what your sanctions will be. Alternatively, you may tell him that you will exercise a sanction, but that you will decide the nature of that sanction only in the event that he breaks the rule. I prefer the latter course, since it gives me more room to manoeuvre (cf. Fisch, Weakland and Segal, 1982). For example, I may tell the person that were he to come to a session under the influence of drink, I would decide at the time whether to go on with the session or require that he came back at a later date when sober.

Steiner's 'Four Requirements'

Claude Steiner (1974) has suggested four requirements for sound contract-making. They are modelled on the practice of contract-making in legal settings. These requirements apply most obviously to the business contract, though they are equally relevant to the treatment contract. All TA practitioners follow Steiner's rules in contract-making. The four requirements are:

- mutual consent
- valid consideration
- competency
- lawful object.

Mutual consent

This means that both you and your client need to agree to the terms of the contract. You thus need to negotiate those terms between you, rather than one party imposing terms on the other. This demands that both of you must make explicit what you want and what you are agreeing.

Valid consideration

Steiner uses the word 'consideration' in its legal sense: it means some kind of recompense paid by one party to another for services rendered. If you are in private practice, the consideration will most often be the fee paid to you by the client. But you may have worked out your own alternatives. For instance, you may provide counselling in return for services in kind. If you are working in an agency, the consideration may come from them and not from the client directly.

You may even decide to work for no tangible reward. In that case you may get your consideration simply in the form of job satisfaction. However, there are risks in working free of charge or at low rates. If you under-charge, you may end up resenting your clients or burning out. Or the client, outside of her awareness, may perceive you as modelling 'I am not important' or 'I am no good at what I do'. If the client's inclination is to model on you, she may take on board the beliefs that *she* is not important or no good. Alternatively, without being consciously aware of it, she may adopt a vengeful posture and set up an outcome in which she 'makes a fool of' you by not changing. Her unspoken perception may be that if you put no value on your own work, you must really *be* worthless. By requiring valid consideration, you help yourself and your client to avoid these pitfalls.

Competency

Competency is required of both you and your client. For you, competency means having the training and skills required to work with this client on this contract. It also means you must provide an appropriate setting. For example, I am not competent to work with children. I have no experience of working with them, and no equipment for specialized techniques such as play therapy.

For the client, competency means the ability to understand the contract negotiation and to take responsibility for his side of the contract. This implies that minors cannot make a competent contract. Neither can persons who are severely brain-damaged or acutely psychotic. If someone is under the influence of drink or mind-altering drugs, she is not competent to enter into a contract.

Lawful object

This implies that everything agreed upon in the contract must be legal. For you it also means that the provisions of the contract must conform to your code of professional ethics.

John: Business Contract

In my work with John, negotiation of the business contract was straightforward. I first stated my rules for working together, and told John that if we fixed an appointment and he did not turn up, I would decide on each occasion what I was going to do about that. I might or might not charge him, depending on what else I did with the time. John agreed to these conditions.

We next agreed to meet for ten once-weekly sessions of fifty minutes each, for which John would pay me at my current fee. The last of these sessions was to be for mutual assessment, after which we might either end counselling or continue if we both so wished.

Self-supervision 5.3

THE BUSINESS CONTRACT

If your chosen client is one whom you are already seeing:

1   Review the rules you have set for working with this client, comparing them with the set of rules given in the section above. Are you satisfied with the protection your rules afford you and your client? What sanctions do you propose to use if the client breaks any of your rules?
2   Review your business contract with this client. How far does it follow Steiner's 'four requirements'? What implications follow for your client and yourself?

If you have chosen to follow the stages of TA treatment through with a new client, devote a session or sessions to setting out your rules and negotiating a business contract that follows Steiner's requirements.

With the business contract complete, you can move into more detailed assessment of your client. You have already met a diagnostic framework that you can use for this purpose: the Racket System. In the coming chapter, we look at ways in which you can compile Racket System information.

EXPLORING A CHILDHOOD LIFE-PLAN

In this chapter, I show how you can compile the details of your client's Racket System. This information will enable you and your client to see how she has been maintaining her problems. The completed Racket System information thus provides you with a 'road map' that you can use in developing a directed plan for treatment.

In Chapter 3 we saw that if the person is to make a lasting move out of script, she must update her *script beliefs* and deal with the associated *script feelings*. This chapter therefore focuses mainly on gathering information about these two elements of the Racket System.

Before reading further, you may wish to review the detail of the Racket System and the life-script (Chapter 3). Here is a brief reminder. The *life-script* is a life-plan that the person writes for herself in childhood. The young child composes the life-script as a set of *script decisions*. She makes these early decisions as a means of surviving and getting needs met in a world that often seems hostile. Script decisions are made partly in response to *script messages* the child receives from parents or parent-figures.

As part of the process of making script decisions, the infant may express feelings but not get her needs met. Over time she learns to employ other feelings as a magical means of extorting attention from her caretakers. She represses her original feeling.

The person may carry script decisions into adulthood in the form of *script beliefs*. These beliefs are normally held outside of awareness. When under stress, the person may begin thinking and acting in ways that are a response to her script beliefs rather than to here-and-now reality. At these times she will also experience the substitute feelings she learned to use in her childhood. These repetitive patterns of scripty behaviours, thoughts and feelings make up the person's *rackety displays*.

This chapter is divided into three main sections. The first section deals with script beliefs. The second covers script feelings and the behaviours that go with them. In the third section we consider the dynamic relationships that may exist between one script belief and another.

Self-supervision 6.1a

DRAWING UP THE RACKET SYSTEM

In this chapter I am suggesting a self-supervision sequence that you can carry out part by part as you read through the chapter.

Take a sheet of paper or use a whiteboard. Draw on it the Racket System diagram shown in Figure 3.1.

On this blank diagram you can compile Racket System data for your chosen client. As you read the material that follows, keep that client in mind. Jot down on the blank diagram whatever detail of script beliefs, rackety displays and so on which you think may apply to that client.

Discovering Script Beliefs

In this section I shall describe how you can compile detail of your client's script beliefs on the evidence of observations you make of her as you work. These include her self-presentation, the type of parenting she received, and the nature of the problem she presents.

How can you tell when your client is replaying a script belief? I think you are best able to detect script beliefs if you know in some detail what script decisions are, and how they are made. This is what I describe in the present section.

There is an important distinction to be made between script beliefs that date from later childhood and those that the person arrived at earlier in life. I shall begin by explaining this distinction.

The Counterscript and the Script Proper

Some of the person's script beliefs will reflect script decisions made in early childhood. Others will relate to decisions made at a later stage of development. There is no moment that forms a sharp dividing line between 'earlier' and 'later' decisions, since the child may make script decisions at any age. Nevertheless, it is usual in TA to make a working distinction between these two categories of decision. This division depends primarily on whether the child made a particular decision before or after she developed a significant command of language. The script beliefs relating to these two types of script decision are manifested in different ways in adult life. Hence when you are compiling them on the Racket System you need to know the different clues to each.

Further, when the child is forming her life-script she may combine earlier and later decisions in various ways. In particular, she may use a later decision as defence against an earlier one. This has direct relevance to your treatment planning, as I explain in the final main section of this chapter.

In standard TA terminology, the set of decisions made in later childhood is known as the *counterscript*, while the earlier decisions make up the *script proper* (Steiner, 1966; Stewart and Joines, 1987: 125–33). I shall go on now to give more detail on these two areas of the life-script, and explain how you can distinguish the script beliefs that relate to each.

Beliefs from Later Childhood: the Counterscript

Counterscript decisions are made relatively late in childhood and are primarily verbal. Thus the grown-up person will usually have little trouble in bringing the corresponding script beliefs into awareness and expressing them in words. Typically, the counterscript contains a huge collection of mottoes, slogans, generalizations and definitions that the person heard in later childhood from parents or parent-figures and uncritically 'swallowed whole' as unquestioned truth. Many of these statements are parental value-judgements. They also include assertions about reality that may be factually true, but may equally well be false or untestable. Examples:

'It's wicked to steal.'
'People who live in glass houses shouldn't throw stones.'
'Eating fish is good for the brain.'
'To show you're a man, you need to drink hard.'
'A woman's place is in the home.'

The person's counterscript will reflect his cultural background as well as his own parenting and schooling. This *cultural scripting* may incorporate racial or social stereotypes, as well as a whole host of behavioural norms that differ from one culture to another (White and White, 1975).

For example, belching at table is 'rude' according to my own British cultural counterscript, whereas in some other cultures it is rude *not* to belch as a signal of appreciation after a good meal.

Importantly also, the counterscript usually contains a set of beliefs that are responses to performance demands, 'dos' and 'don'ts', which the person's parents or parent-figures imposed upon her in later childhood, and which she now continues to impose upon herself. Examples:

'Don't be naughty!'
'Do your best!'
'If at first you don't succeed, try, try, try again!'
'Come top of the class!'
'Be a little ray of sunshine!'

If the child incorporates commands like these into her counterscript, she often frames them as conditions that she believes will determine her acceptability as a person. Suppose, for instance, that a schoolchild frequently hears her parents and teachers demand 'Work hard!' She may form the script belief 'I'm only acceptable if I work hard.' (I am using the word 'acceptable' here in place of the traditional TA term 'OK'.) The grown-up person may interpret 'acceptable' as 'acceptable to others' or 'acceptable to myself'. In either case, the underlying Child motivation is to stay acceptable to the internalized Parent.

For most of the time, people use their counterscript constructively. Counterscript patterns help us adapt comfortably to societal demands without having to think the behaviour out afresh on each occasion (for example, when I obey my self-imposed command 'Don't belch at table!' while eating with other Britons).

However, most people have certain elements of the counterscript which they sometimes use in a way that is negative or painful for them. An example might be the person who received the parental demand 'Come top of the class!' and incorporated it into his counterscript. He might use this self-imposed demand in adult life to become a high achiever in material terms, and do so comfortably. Alternatively, he might use the same demand to goad himself into harmful overwork or physical breakdown.

Recognizing counterscript beliefs

When the grown-up person makes any move that would contradict one of the self-imposed demands in her counterscript, she will often be able to 'hear' in her head the scolding she would have heard as a child had she disobeyed the original demand from the parent. Usually, she will have no difficulty in distinguishing which parent-figure the voice belongs to. For example, about to have sex, she may 'hear' Mother proclaiming: 'Naughty, naughty! Nice girls don't do that!'

In terms of ego-states, you may observe the person expressing counter-script beliefs in two different ways. She may be in her Parent ego-state, quoting mottoes or slogans or making performance demands on others. Alternatively she may speak or act from a Child ego-state in ways that indicate she herself is complying with performance demands or acting in accordance with Parental slogans. In the latter case, she is likely to be carrying on an internal dialogue. She replays the Parental messages internally and complies with them from Child.

When someone says 'you' and means 'I', then what follows is often a statement from the person's counterscript. Example: 'When you don't get things right first time, you should keep on trying, shouldn't you?'

Self-supervision 6.1b

COUNTERSCRIPT BELIEFS

Review the information given above about counterscript beliefs. Relate it to what you know about your chosen client. On the Racket System diagram, fill in your impression of the client's counterscript beliefs. List these separately under the three headings: beliefs about self, about others, about the quality of life.

Beliefs from Early Childhood: the Script Proper

The pre-verbal child thinks, experiences emotions and perceives the world in ways that are markedly different from those of later childhood. This is reflected in certain typical differences between earlier script decisions (script proper) and later decisions (counterscript). There are corresponding differences between the script beliefs dating from earlier and from later childhood. Here are four main characteristics of the script proper, contrasted with those of the counterscript:

1 *Earlier decisions are primarily pre-verbal, while later decisions are primarily verbal.* I have already mentioned that this is the usual rule-of-thumb for distinguishing earlier from later decisions. Because the young child forms her decisions mainly without words, any verbal description can only be an approximation to the child's actual experience. In adult life, the nearest we come to this experience is in our dreams. Vague, changeable images, charged with emotion and unconcerned with the 'logic' of adult waking life – this is the stuff of the child's early decisions.

Indeed, time spent in working with your own dreams gives you a head-start in understanding the nature of early decisions and interpreting the clues to them. As you listen to your client during a counselling session, you can often pick up early script beliefs by paying attention to symbolism, double meanings or plays on words in the same way as you might while working with a dream.

Example: a client and I were discussing his relationship with his father. Though this client was a graduate and held a professional job, he told me that whenever he was with his father he felt tongue-tied, stupid and unable to think clearly. I asked him: 'So what are you scared your father would do if you were to show him you can think clearly?'

My client replied: 'I'm scared he would put me down.'

I asked him to be aware of the phrase 'put down'. As we explored its double meaning, the client uncovered his early childhood belief: not merely that his father might make a fool of him, but that he might kill him.

2 *Earlier decisions are made on the basis of concrete and magical thinking, rather than the 'rational' thinking of the older child or adult.* Research on children's thinking (for example, Piaget, 1951) indicates that the young child usually thinks in concrete terms rather than employing general concepts. She also accepts that things happen by what adults would call 'magic' rather than in the cause-and-effect terms we use in grown-up thinking. You are likely to meet both these features in your clients' early script beliefs.

For example, suppose a young girl has a sister who dies in infancy. She notes that her parents seem to be lavishing much more feeling on her dead sister than they are giving to her. She may then decide without words: 'My sister died and she is getting lots of attention. Therefore, the way to get attention is to die. Therefore, to get back my parents' attention, I'd better die like my sister did.' As a grown-up woman, she may still hold the belief outside of awareness: 'The way for me to get love and attention is to die.'

3   *Early decisions are often global and sweeping, while later decisions are more limited in scope.* This point relates closely to the last. Recall from Chapter 3 that the young child makes script decisions as a way of getting by as best she can in a world that may seem hostile. Unable to understand the complex nature of cause and effect, she does not make her decisions in terms of 'I'd better be careful not to ...' or 'I'd better check before doing ...'. Instead she is likely to make sweeping decisions like 'On no account must I ever again ...' or 'For the rest of my life, I'll be ...'.

For example, suppose a little boy experiences inconsistent parenting from his mother. Sometimes when he cries for her, she comes and is affectionate to him. At other times she does not come at all. At still other times, she comes but is rough and angry with him. The infant may then decide, not merely 'I can't trust Mother', but 'Never again will I trust anybody.' As a grown-up man he may still be acting upon his global belief: 'Nobody can be trusted.'

4   *Earlier decisions are often seen by the infant as necessary to ensure survival or avoid disaster.* This contrasts with the less extreme way in which the older child may view his counterscript decisions, as being necessary to ensure his personal acceptability. Fanita English (1977) uses the graphic term 'survival conclusions' to describe the child's earlier decisions.

We need to bear in mind that the young child's concept of 'survival' may not be the same as that of the grown-up person or older child. To the infant, survival may imply keeping the love and attention of the parents, rather than avoiding the physical event of death. I have already given an example in which the child decided: 'To keep my parents' attention, I need to die.' Where the young child frames the early decision as being a magical defence against disaster, the disaster in question may be total abandonment or engulfment by the parent (Gobes, 1985); or the infant may simply fear some unspeakable catastrophe that must be guarded against at all costs.

Recognizing beliefs from earlier childhood

This gives you one way of recognizing when the person is replaying early script beliefs in grown-up life. Suppose the adult person is about to act in some way that would be in conflict with one of his early survival conclusions. Outside of his awareness in Child, he registers an immediate risk of disaster. He is likely to respond by feeling physical distress or emotional discomfort.

For example, suppose a little boy makes the decision 'Never again will I get close to anyone, because if I do, I risk being swallowed up.' Now suppose that years later, as a grown-up man, he hears someone ask him 'Will you give me a hug?' He may begin sweating, feel his heart race or his stomach knot up. As he does so, he is likely to remain unaware that he is responding to his own belief: 'It's disastrous to get physically close.'

This physical and emotional experience differs from that which the person is likely to report if he goes against one of his counterscript beliefs (see the previous section).

In terms of ego-state shifts, you may observe both Parent and Child clues that the person is replaying a belief from the script proper. As compared with the clues to a counterscript belief, the Parent here is likely to sound much harsher and more punitive. This is because this Parent is a fantasized one that the person constructed for himself at a relatively early stage of development. In Child, the person will re-enact behaviours that also date from this earlier stage of life. He may express magical beliefs and catastrophic fears. The issues for this Child will be survival, self-worth and getting basic needs met.

Twelve Common Script Beliefs

The detailed content of the script proper is unique to each individual. However, certain broad themes turn up again and again in the analysis of these script beliefs from early childhood. Robert and Mary Goulding (1976, 1979) have distinguished twelve of these themes, developed from their experience as psychotherapists.

In their original work, the Gouldings phrased these twelve script themes in terms of the restrictive script *messages* that the young child receives from the parent. To convey this they began each message with the word 'Don't ...', for example, 'Don't Exist.' Here I am primarily focusing on the *decisions* the child makes in obeying these messages. It is these decisions that the person may carry into adulthood as script *beliefs*. Thus instead of 'Don't ...' I shall write 'I Mustn't ...', for example, 'I Mustn't Exist'. With this amendment, the Gouldings' list is as follows:

- I Mustn't Exist.
- I Mustn't Be Me.
- I Mustn't Be a Child.
- I Mustn't Grow Up.
- I Mustn't Make It.

- I Mustn't Do Anything.
- I Mustn't Be Important.
- I Mustn't Belong.
- I Mustn't Be Close.
- I Mustn't Be Well (I Mustn't Be Sane).
- I Mustn't Think.
- I Mustn't Feel.

The person who makes any of these decisions in childhood may carry it forward into adult life as a script belief. As you compile the detail of your client's Racket System, it is useful to listen in particular for clues to these twelve common beliefs.

In the coming subsections I describe typical clues to each belief. These clues include patterns of difficulty and self-restriction that are expressions of the belief in question. The person may also report particular ways in which she experienced her parents during her childhood.

I mustn't exist

Usually, the infant decides I Mustn't Exist when she perceives her parent as wishing her dead. The detailed content of the decision may take various different forms, for example:

'I don't deserve to live.'
'If I die, maybe Mother will love me.'
'I'll kill myself to get you.'
'I'll get you to kill me.'

Decisions like these may imply a tragic script outcome of suicide (Chapters 3 and 7). Alternatively the infant may make the magical decision that she can avoid killing herself if she kills somebody else instead, or that she can stay alive if she ceases to exist as a thinking person, that is, goes crazy.

In the adult person, typical clues to the script belief I Mustn't Exist are:

- attempted suicide
- actual or attempted physical self-harm
- actual or attempted physical harm of others
- thoughts or fantasies of physically harming self or others
- physically harmful addiction or substance abuse

- mannerisms indicating self-harm, for example, hitting self
- feelings of worthlessness, of being unwanted or unloved
- reports of physical abuse by parents
- memories of parental statements such as: 'Drop dead', 'I wish I'd never had you', 'You hurt me when you were born', 'If it hadn't been for you, I could have ... .'
- death of a sibling in the person's early childhood
- unwillingness to 'close escape hatches' (see Chapter 7).

A surprisingly large proportion of clients reveal I Mustn't Exist as one of their script beliefs. However, relatively few of them actually attempt suicide. This is because people are ingenious at constructing conditional defences against the suicidal payoff. The form of this defence is to decide 'I can keep on existing *so long as I* ... '. I discuss this in more detail in the final main section of this chapter.

I mustn't be me

Here the parent stops short of wanting the child dead. Instead she wishes he were a different child. Where the parents wanted a girl but had a boy, or vice versa, the infant's decision may take the form 'I Mustn't Be the Sex I Am.' Indications of this script belief may be:

- estimation of self as inferior to others (these may be specific others who were favoured during the person's childhood)
- behaviour or choice of dress typical of the other sex
- memories of a sibling or another child being consistently praised or favoured in preference to the client
- memories of parental statements like 'We always wanted a girl/boy, but you came along instead'.

Supporting evidence may be that the parents gave the child a name that is ambiguous as to gender, for example, a girl named Pat or Jacky, a boy named Evelyn or Vivian.

I mustn't be a child

The child may make this decision where the parent – in his own Child ego-state – sees his son or daughter as potential competition for a limited amount of love. Alternatively, the parent may have grown up in a restrictive home where he was not allowed to be childlike. Outside of awareness, he now may feel bitterly jealous of his own offspring getting the fun and freedom he missed himself. Where the person grows to adulthood still harbouring the script belief I Mustn't Be a Child, you may observe him showing clues such as:

- habitual stiffness and solemnity in manner
- awkwardness in dealing with children
- discomfort in situations that entail playing, behaving spontaneously or having fun, particularly where there are no rules
- memories of parental statements like 'Children should be seen and not heard'
- memories of parents being angry at playful or spontaneous behaviour.

Eldest children and only children are especially likely to have decided I Mustn't Be a Child.

I mustn't grow up

Conversely, I Mustn't Grow Up is often decided upon by the youngest child in a family. Here the child's parent may be conveying from her own Child ego-state 'Don't leave me!' This may be because the parent sees the child as her only source of playful companionship. Other parents may be fearful of the void that they believe will open up when their last child leaves home. When someone believes I Mustn't Grow Up, you may notice:

- habitual childlike mannerisms
- avoidance of positions of responsibility
- inclination for relationships where the other person takes charge
- readiness to escalate feelings in response to stress
- discomfort in situations that call for analysis or self-restraint, especially when this entails setting rules for self or others.

The person who decided I Mustn't Grow Up may stay at home in adulthood to become caretaker to an aged parent. Another interpretation of this belief is 'I Mustn't Be Sexy'.

I mustn't make it

This decision is typically made by the child whose parent feels threatened by his son's or daughter's achievement. Without awareness, the parent may feel in her own Child ego-state 'I never ... (had a good education, a good job, praise for skills at sport and so on). So I'm damned if my child is going to have it now!'

In adult life the belief I Mustn't Make It often surfaces as a habitual pattern of self-sabotage. This may emerge especially when the person is 'in danger of' making some important achievement. For instance, a student may get good marks in term-time essays, then go blank in the middle of a crucial examination. Another frequent mode of self-sabotage is to contract some kind of psychosomatic illness.

Sometimes the early decision I Mustn't Make It is combined with a later (counterscript) decision such as 'I have to work hard.' From Parent, the parent wants his child to succeed, while from Child he wants her to fail. The combination of the two messages presents the child with a double bind. In response, she may decide 'To get my parent's love, I need to work hard but fail at things.'

I mustn't do anything

The child makes this decision in response to non-verbal messages from the parent that convey 'Don't do anything, because anything you do is so dangerous that you'd better do nothing at all.' Indications of the script belief in grown-up life are:

- maladaptive over-cautiousness
- habitual dithering between courses of action
- never getting started on projects
- 'Damned if I do, damned if I don't'.

I mustn't be important

This decision also is a response to the parent's feelings of competition with his offspring. The parent enjoins from Child 'It's OK for you to be around, son or daughter, but only if you realize you and your wants are not important.' Patterns emerging in adult life may be:

- wanting things but not asking for them openly
- unease in leadership situations
- difficulty speaking in public
- feelings of insignificance
- experience of being one-down to authority figures.

I mustn't belong

The early decision I Mustn't Belong shows up in adult life as a sensation of being 'out of it' in groups. The person will typically find ways of engineering this experience in all sorts of different groups. For example, she may attend an evening class and feel she is being excluded from the conversation because she is out of her depth intellectually. Then she goes home and feels isolated from her family because they can't understand the subject she has been studying in the class.

I Mustn't Belong is often modelled for the child by parents who themselves have trouble in relating to groups.

I mustn't be close

This decision also is often a response to parental modelling. It may be interpreted as 'I Mustn't Get Close Physically' or 'I Mustn't Make Emotional Contact'. A variant is 'I Mustn't Trust.'

Sometimes the child may make one of these decisions when he experiences his parent as being inconsistent in showing feelings. For example, when the infant asks Mother for affection she may respond on one occasion, ignore him next time, and be angry with him on a third occasion. The child may then decide: 'I can't trust the way people respond when I get close. Therefore, it's safer not to get close at all.' Clues to this script belief in adulthood may include:

* unease at touching or being touched
* lack of emotional rapport with family or friends
* difficulty in giving or receiving affection
* unwillingness to enter committed relationships.

I mustn't be well (I mustn't be sane)

This may be modelled by a parent who uses illness or craziness as a means of manipulating people. Often, however, the child makes this decision when her parents provide her with more warm caring when she is ill than when she is well. The variant I Mustn't Be Sane may sometimes be decided upon by the child in response to an unspoken 'family curse' whereby all children of a particular name, position in the family and so on are expected to go crazy.

You will recall that a script outcome of 'go crazy' can also reflect the childhood decision I Mustn't Exist. If in doubt whether the person's script belief is I Mustn't Exist or I Mustn't Be Sane, always assume the former.

I mustn't think

The young child may decide I Mustn't Think when the parent consistently belittles the child's thinking ability. The decision may also be a response to modelling. For instance, a mother may model for her daughter how to manipulate for what she wants by turning off her thinking and escalating feelings instead. As clues to the belief I Mustn't Think, you may observe:

- habitual 'blanking out' or confusion when faced with problems
- escalating feelings as a substitute for thinking
- use of phrases such as 'I can't think', 'I've gone blank', 'My mind must be going'.

I mustn't feel

This may imply 'I Mustn't Feel Emotions' or 'I Mustn't Feel Sensations'. The child may make the decision to blank out all emotions or sensations, or only specified ones. For example, she may decide 'I won't let myself feel angry' or 'I won't let myself feel whether my stomach is full or empty'. The decision I Mustn't Feel may be a response to parental modelling. Often particular emotions or sensations are prohibited in the family. Clues to the script belief I Mustn't Feel in the adult person include:

- reports of never feeling ... (angry, sad, scared and so on)
- reports that one or both parents never showed ... (anger, sadness and so on)
- behaviour patterns that entail blanking off physical sensations, for example, habitual overeating or undereating.

Self-supervision 6.1c

THE SCRIPT PROPER

Review the clues to beliefs from the script proper that have been given in the sections above. Which of these clues does your client show?

On this evidence, make your initial assessment of the beliefs in your client's script proper. Once again, enter them on the Racket System diagram under the headings for self, others and the quality of life.

John: Script Beliefs

In my work with John, I drew up an initial picture of his Racket System as we spoke together over several sessions after completing intake. I shared my thinking with John and compiled the information in co-operation with him. The results were written up on a Racket System diagram that I drew out on a flip-chart sheet and kept in view during these early sessions. Throughout our work together, we referred back to the Racket System framework. As John brought to light more features of his script, we revised and added to the detail on the Racket System.

While we were doing this I emphasized to John that the map we were drawing was one that *he could change* if he wanted to change it. I made clear that it was *not* intended as a statement of 'how this person is and always will be'. Instead, its purpose was to discover how John *had been*, and help him answer the interesting question of how he *might choose to be* in the future. Later, when John was ready to begin active change, we would keep track of his movement out of script by examining what parts of the Racket System he had updated.

I judged that two of John's counterscript beliefs were 'To be acceptable, I have to get everything right' and 'To be acceptable, I must disown my feelings and wants'. He frequently felt anxious in the company of Helen's family in case he was 'getting things wrong' socially in some unspecified way. One of the difficulties in his relationships with women, he told me, was that he had had difficulty in telling them how he felt or what he wanted from them.

From John's overall presentation and on the evidence of the problems he reported, I judged that three of his beliefs from early childhood were:

'I Mustn't Be a Child (I Mustn't Enjoy Anything).'
'I Mustn't Be Close (I Must Never Trust Anybody).'
'I Mustn't Feel (any other feeling than anger).'

From the second of these beliefs about self there followed related beliefs about others:

'Other people can't be trusted',

and a belief about the quality of life:

'Life is unpredictable and unfair.'

John's depressed mother had been slightly shadowy in his child-hood. His childhood history was dominated by his overbearing father, who had been physically violent against his wife and John, as well as John's brothers. The violence confirmed that John's father had given him the script message 'Don't Exist'. I judged that John had accepted this command in his early years, and so I added to his Racket System the belief 'I Mustn't Exist'. This, in any case, had already been indi-cated in the here-and-now by John's own use of violence.

I noted that there was a script message that John had received from both parents: 'Don't Be Close.' For both parents, this trans-lated both as 'Don't be close physically or emotionally' and 'Don't trust'. I guessed therefore that John's script beliefs around these two messages would need particular attention in the process of change. In the counselling relationship, it was likely that John would soon be busy testing me for trustworthiness. And I guessed that, as in his infancy, he might want to 'test to destruction': to try our relation-ship more and more sorely until he got me to reject him. If he did test me in this way, my response would be: 'I don't like the way you're pushing me, but I'm not going to reject you.' By this means I would convey to John in his Child that his *behaviour* was unwel-come to me, but that *he* was still OK by me as a person. As it was, his script belief had been the opposite. He had been believing: 'I'm essentially unlovable. Therefore, people will reject me for what I am, not for what I do.'

Both John's parents had modelled for John their own script belief: 'The way to resolve disputes is to be violent.' I guessed that John had been replaying this pattern in his relationships: feeling angry, bottling up his anger for a while, then expressing it explo-sively in violence. One of my tasks in counselling would be to help John find an appropriate Adult means of settling conflicts that did not entail hitting people. Along the way, this would probably mean his learning to express anger non-destructively when he felt it, rather than storing it up.

Rackety Displays

In this second main section of the chapter, we go on to look at how you can compile information about your client's rackety displays. In the same way as in the previous section, I shall begin by explaining what these patterns are and how they originate. You can use this knowledge when you are investigating rackety displays in practice.

Rackets and Racket Feelings

Every child discovers that some feelings are prohibited in his family, while others are rewarded. If he expresses the prohibited feelings, he does not get his needs met. He soon becomes skilled at blanking off these forbidden feelings. He discovers that by showing the family's favoured feelings instead, he can often get the attention he seeks (English, 1971, 1972). Soon he has worked out patterns of thinking and behaviour that he uses to 'justify' feeling these favoured emotions.

As an adult, he may react to stress by re-running his old patterns and feeling the emotions he decided 'got results' for him as a child. In TA these repetitive patterns of thinking and behaviour are called *rackets*. The learned feelings that go with them are called *racket feelings*.

Key Ideas 6.1

RACKETS AND RACKET FEELINGS

1   A *racket feeling* is a familiar emotion, learned and encouraged in childhood. In adult life the person may experience the racket feeling in many different stress situations.

2   A racket feeling always acts as a *substitute* for another feeling that was prohibited in the family of origin.

3   A *racket* is a set of thoughts and behaviours intended outside awareness as a means of 'justifying' the person in experiencing a racket feeling. When in script, the person will show these thoughts and behaviours repetitively.

4   Each time the person perceives others as stroking her for a racket or for the expression of a racket feeling, she will interpret this in Child as confirmation of her script beliefs.

Discovering rackets and racket feelings

Here is a sequence of questions that you can put to your client as a way of finding out about his rackets and racket feelings. Note the answer to each question before going on to the next.

- When things go wrong for you, how do you usually feel? *(This question is worded in a way that invites report of a racket feeling.)*
- Do you recognize this as a familiar feeling of yours?
- Is it a feeling you experience in response to a wide range of different situations?
- When did you last feel this feeling?
- What was the situation in which you felt it? *(This invites a report of the racket.)*
- With hindsight, how far would you say you had a part in setting up that situation (though you might not have been aware of doing so at the time)?
- Did the feeling you felt help you to get your needs met in the here-and-now?
- When you were a child, was this feeling favoured or rewarded in your family?
- Suppose you were using this favoured feeling to cover up another feeling that was prohibited or punished when you were a child; what would you guess is this original feeling you were covering up?

If the person did in some way help set up the stress situation in which he felt a racket feeling, then the thinking and behaviour he employed to set it up will be one of his rackets. This may entail interactions with others (see *racketeering* and *games*, described below and in Chapter 9). Alternatively the person may set up a racket single-handed. For example, someone may habitually 'lose' his wallet, tell himself he'll be in bad trouble if he can't find it, and feel panicky. A single-handed racket may sometimes be purely a matter of internal dialogue. For example, when carrying out some work assignment, the person may tell himself from Parent 'I'm not doing this as well as I should be!' He thus 'justifies' experiencing a racket feeling of inadequacy in Child.

Racket Feelings and Authentic Feelings

Berne (1966: 308–9) chose the word 'racket' to underline the manipulative nature of these substitute emotions. But this is not to say that racket feelings are *experienced* as 'phoney' by the person who feels them. When I feel a racket feeling, I am in no doubt that my feeling is 'real'. Thus to express the idea of 'feelings that are not racket feelings', we speak of *authentic feelings* rather than 'real feelings'.

By the time a person reaches adulthood, he has repressed the entire racket process from his awareness. Suppose he goes into script under stress. He is then likely to begin experiencing his authentic childhood emotion. But, in the manner of a 'conditioned reflex', he will switch immediately into the racket feeling as he replays his script beliefs (recall the Racket System, Chapter 3). We say the person *covers* the authentic feeling with the racket feeling. Usually the switch into the racket feeling is made so quickly that the person is not aware of having felt the authentic emotion.

Distinguishing racket feelings from authentic feelings

In TA it is usual to list four authentic emotions:

* anger
* sadness
* fear
* happiness.

Often we simply say 'mad, sad, scared or glad'.

Thus if the person is experiencing any other emotion than those four, you know that emotion is a racket feeling. The rationale for this is that these four emotions are the ones that an infant feels before he has any concept of censoring.

There is a complication, however. Anger, sadness, fear and happiness are not *always* authentic. They may also be experienced as racket feelings. Indeed, a person may switch from moment to moment between the authentic and rackety versions of any of these four emotions.

How can you tell the difference between the authentic versions of these feelings and their rackety counterparts? Often you can tell from context. If the person experiences a particular emotion *repetitively*, in a wide range of different situations, it is most likely to be a racket feeling.

While there are only four names for authentic emotions, racket feelings have innumerable different names to describe them. Some racket feelings are experienced from a one-down position. Examples: frustration, guilt, embarrassment, anxiety, jealousy, helplessness, despair. Others reflect a one-up stance. Examples: blamefulness, blamelessness, condescension, contempt.

Not all racket feelings are experienced as unpleasant, either by those who feel them or by others. For example, a little girl may learn that she is not supposed to show anger. Instead, she is rewarded for being bubbly, bright and cheerful. As a grown-up woman, she may continue to get recognition for being 'everybody's ray of sunshine'. Her racket feelings are happiness and excitement. She uses them to cover the authentic anger that was a forbidden feeling in childhood, and which she is still forbidding herself to feel as an adult.

The problem-solving function of feelings

Thomson (1983) points out that authentic fear, anger and sadness have a *problem-solving* function. By contrast, racket feelings are ineffective as a grown-up means of solving problems. This is another clue by which you can distinguish between racket and authentic feelings.

It may seem odd at first to suggest that people can solve problems by expressing feelings. Thomson explains as follows:

* Authentic *anger* helps solve problems in the *present*. For example, if someone elbows me rudely, I can regain my space by expressing anger appropriate to the situation and elbowing him back.
* Authentic *sadness* helps solve problems from the *past*. If I have been bereaved or have suffered an irreversible loss, I heal myself by the process of mourning.
* Authentic *fear* helps solve problems that are likely to arise in the *future*. Walking city streets at night, I may consider taking a short-cut through a dark alley. But, feeling scared, I stay in the well-lit streets to avoid potential danger.

Stewart and Joines (1987) extend Thomson's scheme by suggesting that authentic *happiness* signals: 'All's well, no change needed.'

This offers you still another means of distinguishing authentic anger, sadness, fear and happiness from their rackety counterparts. If one of these feelings is felt *outside its appropriate time-frame*, then it is likely to be a racket feeling.

Example: an adult person may experience anger at his mother for not loving him more while he was a child. But no matter how angry he feels, he will never bring his childhood back. The authentic feeling in this example would be sadness. By letting himself mourn the love he will now never get, he can free himself to seek love from others in the present.

Why are racket feelings ineffectual as an adult means of problem-solving? When someone experiences a racket feeling, he is in script. Outside of awareness, he hopes his feeling will manipulate support from others in the way he perceived it doing when he was an infant. If others react in a way that seems to fulfil this hope, the person may feel temporary satisfaction. But his underlying Child need has not been met. He has still not expressed the authentic feeling that would let others know what that need is.

Consider the woman in the earlier example, who covers her anger with racket happiness. Each time she does this, she may get smiles from her family and feel satisfied for a while. But she has done nothing to resolve whatever intrusion, attack or insult she is feeling angry about. Thus it will not be long before she begins to get back in touch with her anger. The moment she does so she will switch back to the racket feeling, and unless this is confronted, she will be ready to replay the whole process.

Discovering authentic feelings

In the set of questions you asked to discover your client's rackets and racket feelings (see above) you ended with the question 'What feeling do you guess you may have been covering up?'

In answer, the client may have reported anger, sadness, fear or happiness. These may be either racket or authentic feelings. Alternatively, she may have named one of the many other emotions that always signify racket feelings. In either case, you may follow up with a question that invites a report of the authentic feeling. Ask 'How do you feel about feeling ... *(name the feeling she has reported)?*'

When the client replies, repeat the same question. Continue until she names one of the four authentic feelings and stays with the same feeling even when you repeat the question. Suppose the client has reported that, at the end of some recent scene, he felt indignant at someone else. You might go on:

COUNSELLOR: So suppose for a moment that when you felt indignant, there was some other feeling you were covering up. If there was another feeling, what do you guess it would be?

CLIENT: I suppose I felt powerless.

COUNSELLOR: And how do you feel about feeling powerless?

CLIENT: I feel angry.

COUNSELLOR: Who do you feel angry at?
CLIENT: Myself.
COUNSELLOR: So how do you feel about feeling angry at yourself?
CLIENT: [Pause] Scared.
COUNSELLOR: And how do you feel about feeling scared?
CLIENT: I don't change my feeling when you ask that. I feel scared.

Self-supervision 6.2a

RACKET FEELINGS AND AUTHENTIC FEELINGS

Review the information in the sections above on racket feelings and authentic feelings. Relate this to your chosen client. You may rely on the knowledge you already have of him, or back this up by using the sequence of questions described.

Bear in mind that the person may show a whole range of behaviours and feelings that are *not* part of the Racket System. Enter as 'rackety displays' only those behaviours and feelings that are *repetitive* and that serve to justify the person's script beliefs or defend against them (Zalcman, 1986).

Enter first any *observable behaviours* the client has reported in the situation where he plays out his racket. What do other people see and hear him doing and saying? What feelings do they note him expressing?

Under 'reported internal experiences', record any emotion he reports *experiencing* during the situation. This may or may not be the same as the emotion he is *expressing*.

Note down also any physical sensations he reports. These may include tension or pain in some part of the body, racing pulse, nausea, warmth, numbness and so on. If he mentions somatic manifestations like indigestion or migraine, record them here also.

If you have traced the client's authentic feeling, note it down in the left-hand column of the Racket System diagram under 'Feelings repressed at time of script decision'.

Racketeering and Games

The terms *racketeering* and *games* both describe ways in which a person repetitively sets up to experience racket feelings through interacting with others. I shall introduce both ideas briefly here to enable you to plot them with other rackety displays on the client's Racket System. In Chapter 9 we shall look at racketeering and games in more detail and consider how to confront them.

Racketeering

The term 'racketeering' was coined by Fanita English (1976a, 1976b). In a racketeering exchange, one person expresses a racket feeling in the hope that the other person will stroke him for it. If the stroke is forthcoming, the racketeer continues to express the same racket feeling in the hope of further strokes. This may continue indefinitely, until the racketeer is temporarily satisfied with the strokes he has gained for his racket feeling.

The Child motivation for racketeering is not only to gain strokes but also to seek 'confirmation' of script beliefs. Each time the listener strokes the racketeer for expressing the racket feeling, the racketeer construes this as supporting his script beliefs. This motivation is outside of the awareness of either person. Thus racketeering always entails the communication of *ulterior messages* (recall Chapter 1).

Example: a client comes into a counselling session and begins telling you at length how angry he is at his wife. He does not mention doing anything to resolve whatever he is angry about. His ulterior invitation to you from Child is: 'Please spend the session offering me sympathetic strokes for my racket anger.'

If two people racketeer together, one will typically take a one-down position, coming from the Child ego-state. The other will assume a one-up stance from Parent.

Games

A game opens in the same way as a racketeering exchange. The parties' exchange ulterior messages and express racket feelings. In a game, however, this does not continue indefinitely. Instead, one of the parties abruptly changes her ground. If she started by racketeering from a one-down position, she suddenly shifts to one-up, and vice versa. In doing so she invites the other person to shift also, and to take up a new complementary role.

English (1976a) suggests a possible Child motivation for this shift in roles. During the original racketeering exchange, one of the parties may begin to get tired of the racketeering and seek to withdraw before the other person feels ready. In that case, the one who does *not* want to withdraw may begin feeling scared in Child that her source of strokes is going to be taken away. Without awareness, she makes the sudden shift of role as a means of keeping the other person around and gaining a renewed supply of strokes.

Berne (1972) used the term *Switch* to describe this abrupt change in roles. Some current TA writers suggest that the Switch be regarded as the defining feature of a game. The presence of the Switch then distinguishes games from racketeering (Joines, 1982; cf. Zalcman, 1987).

I would guess that in your counselling work you may often have heard people say:

'I felt bad about this last time, and now I've gone and done it again.'
'Why does this always happen to me?'
'I thought he was different from all the others, but ... .'

The recurring theme of these complaints is: 'I hated this last time, so why on earth have I just done it again?'

It is the Switch that accounts for this paradoxical déjà vu quality of games. Until the moment of the Switch, the player remains unaware that he is going through the repetitive stages of the game.

Immediately following the Switch, the person experiences a momentary sense of confusion, as he says to himself 'How on earth did I get here again?'

The final step in the game is that the player experiences intense racket feelings. From the start of the whole process, his Child motivation outside of awareness has been to reap this racket-feeling harvest. Berne (1972) called this the *payoff* of the game. At the same time, the person internally restates his script beliefs about himself, the other person, and life in general.

John: Games

In his relationships with women, John had been playing out a game sequence that extended over a long period, lasting two or three years. Here is how the typical stages would go:

1 John assertively pursues a new woman and seduces her. His arrogant social-level message is 'I'm God's gift to women!' Below this on the psychological level, his non-verbal signals convey 'I'm desperately scared because I feel I'm not lovable, and I *know*

you're going to reject me.' This ulterior message is the invitation he offers the other person to enter a game.

2 Like anyone who is playing a game, John has an uncanny ability to seek out relationships with people whose favourite games *interlock* with his own. On the social level, the woman John chooses is long-suffering and undemanding. Outside of her own awareness, though, she is signalling to John 'So you're going to test me to see if I reject you? OK, come on then – you'll find out how hard I can kick!' With this ulterior message, she accepts John's invitation into game-playing.

3 For John and his partner, the next stage of the game typically lasts months or years. On the social level, John comes from a one-up 'macho' position. He sleeps around with other women, picks arguments with his partner and her family. The woman stays in a one-down role, patiently putting up with all his provocations. The more she seems determined to stay close to John, the more severely he tests her. He escalates to physical violence, pushing his partner around or even hitting her.

4 Eventually John's partner pulls the Switch. Shifting from one-down to one-up, she walks out on John without warning. Rejected and left alone, he now makes his own Switch from one-up to one-down.

5 With a sickening sense of 'having been here before', John asks himself 'How on earth did *this* happen to me again?' Meanwhile his one-time partner is experiencing a similar sense of the unexpected, as she muses 'I thought John might be different – why didn't I see he was just the same as all the others?'

6 John feels racket feelings of helplessness, unwantedness and depression. Outside of awareness, he tells himself in his head 'Yes, I was right all along. I *am* unlovable. So that explains why all important women reject me.' His ex-partner experiences familiar feelings of righteous indignation and grim satisfaction, along with a certain sense of guilt. She repeats her script belief without awareness: 'Yes, all men *are* out to take advantage of you. So that's why they deserve to be rejected.'

Each time John and his partner repeat this sequence, they are both re-playing childhood strategies outside of their awareness. These strategies seemed to them in infancy to be a second-best way of getting by in a bad situation. But they still left their original needs unmet. This is why, in adulthood, John and his partner have repeatedly sought out people with whom they can play out their game sequence. They are attempting to satisfy the needs they did not have satisfied in their infancy. But because they are using the same strategies as they did when they were children, they necessarily also get the same unsatisfactory results. The need remains unmet, and the person is set to repeat the whole process of the game.

Games can be played over the long term, as in this example, or over shorter spans of time.

Fantasies and Memories

To complete the Racket System, you can enter details of your client's scripty fantasies and reinforcing memories. Here is a technique developed by Marilyn Zalcman (1986) for gathering this information.

Ask the client to recall a scene in which he experienced whatever problem he has brought to counselling. This is likely to be a scene in which he played out a racket or game and felt racket feelings. If the client is willing, invite him to re-experience the scene rather than simply recalling it. He can do this by telling the scene in the present tense.

Scripty fantasies

When in script, the person may fantasize events that either 'justify' the script beliefs and feelings or defend against them. To investigate these fantasies, you may ask the following question as the client continues to imagine his scene:

'In this situation, what do you feel is the very worst that could happen?'

Record the answer to this, then ask:

'And in this situation, what do you feel is the very best that could happen?'

Usually, the fantasies of both 'worst' and 'best' belong in the Racket System.

Reinforcing memories

You will enter your client's reinforcing memories in the right-hand column of the Racket System. These memories may be either real or imaginary. For the purposes of compiling Racket System data, there is no need to ask your client to distinguish between the two. In either case the client, when in script, will have been selecting these memories to fit with the script beliefs and 'justify' the rackety displays.

Ask your client in the imagined scene: 'What other events have there been in your life that remind you of this scene?'

Follow up with questions to explore what is similar between the original imagined scene and the other scenes now recalled. Relevant scenes will be those in which the client felt the same emotion as in the first scene and behaved in similar repetitive ways.

The final step in the questionnaire is to explore the feedback loop that runs from the reinforcing memories back to the script beliefs. Ask your client: 'So what do these memories demonstrate to you about yourself/about others/about life in general?' As usual, record the answer to each part of the question before going on to the next part.

The Dynamics of the Script

In compiling the Racket System, you have listed the set of script beliefs that the person may need to update in achieving the personal changes she desires. But there is one further piece of information you need before inviting your client to begin making that change in counselling. That is: in what ways has the person been *combining* her various script beliefs?

When a child is composing her life-script, she does not keep each individual script decision isolated from all the others. Instead, she ingeniously tests out combinations of different decisions, continually seeking the best ways of surviving and getting her needs met. Thus the life-script is not a rigid structure built up from isolated units. Rather it is a dynamic, interactive system. If one element of the system is changed, other elements are likely to change in response.

The adult person's script beliefs represent the set of script decisions carried forward from childhood. These do not become fossilized as the person grows up, but retain their dynamic character. Thus as you construct your treatment plan, you continually need to consider the question 'If the client makes *this* change, what other dynamic changes might follow from it?'

One Decision Defending against Another

The young child is ingenious in finding ways to defend against the impact of negative script messages she receives from her parents (Goulding and Goulding, 1979). Sometimes she may simply ignore the message, realizing even at her early age that it reflects her parents' problems rather than her own.

Another frequent way of defending against a destructive message is to make a *compound decision*. Its general form is: 'I can avoid obeying this destructive message *so long as* I obey another of my parents' messages that is a bit less destructive.'

For example, suppose an infant perceives her mother as giving her the message 'I'd rather you were dead'. If the child were to obey this message as it stands, she would simply make the decision I Mustn't Exist.

However, the child is likely to cast around for ways of staying alive. Suppose she also experiences her mother as signalling to her: 'You and your needs are not important to me.' Without words, the child may come to the conclusion: 'It's painful to me that I'm not important to Mother. But maybe at least if I act very unimportant, it'll be OK with her if I keep on living.'

As usual with early decisions, the child is likely to put this in sweeping, global terms. Her compound decision thus becomes: 'It's OK for me to exist *so long as* I stay unimportant to people.'

Thus in this example the child employs I Mustn't Be Important as a magical, conditional defence against the more destructive decision I Mustn't Exist. Note that this compound decision can be re-phrased as:

'If I let myself become important to anyone, I'll drop dead.'

This wording probably gives a better sense of what this kind of compound decision means to the Child.

The infant's compound decisions may include various combinations of the twelve early decisions I have listed in a previous section of this chapter. However, in the great majority of cases the function of the compound decision is to defend against I Mustn't Exist.

Counterscript defending against script proper

Often also, the child may construct a compound decision that uses a counterscript decision as defence against a decision from the script proper. Take once again the example of an infant who makes the early decision I Mustn't Exist. If he manages to postpone carrying out this decision and reaches his later childhood, he may then note that he seems to be acceptable to his parents so long as he works hard. His compound decision then may be 'I can keep on living *so long as* I work hard.'

Again the full implications of this become clearer on re-phrasing: 'If I stop working hard, I'll die.'

The person may then carry this compound decision forward into adult life as a compound script belief.

Compound beliefs in adult life

Consider this person who has made the compound decision in childhood 'If I stop working hard, I'll die.' Consciously, he is unaware that he is still holding to this as a script belief. But he is aware of being uncomfortable at his pattern of overworking, which he 'can't seem to give up'. Now he comes to you for help.

If you did not know about his compound script belief, you might assume that he could break his habit of overwork by making some simple behavioural change. For example, you might invite him to delegate some work or take a holiday.

Yet what would this mean for the client in Child? If he were to make these changes, he would no longer be behaving in accord with his belief 'I have to work hard'. This would mean he had taken away the 'magical defence' he has been using since childhood to avoid his earlier decision not to exist.

What would be likely to happen if your client did go ahead and ease up on work? For a while he might relish his new leisure. But soon he might start feeling bored or depressed, reporting he 'had too much time on his hands'. He might find pretexts for getting back to work, or might fill his spare time with unpaid commitments.

It might appear on the face of it as though your client were 'sabotaging' constructive change. But from the point of view of the client in Child, this would not be 'sabotage' at all. It would be an urgent attempt to ward off annihilation.

Implications for Treatment Direction

Whenever the person is using one script belief as a defence against another, it is likely that the problem he first brings to counselling will reflect the belief that is *being used as the defence*, not the belief that is *being defended against*.

In the example above, your client was using the belief 'I'm acceptable so long as I work hard' as a defence against the earlier belief 'I Mustn't Exist'. Yet he came to you because he was uncomfortable about overworking, not because he was contemplating suicide.

Similarly in the previous example: the person who decided in childhood 'I can stay alive so long as I don't become important' is likely to come to counselling initially because she has intractable problems in asking for what she wants or dealing with authority figures, not because she feels suicidal.

Ideally in cases like these you will plan your treatment sequence so as to *begin* by addressing the script belief against which the person has been defending. In the example of the client who had been overworking, this means that as soon as you and he have agreed a contract for change, you will begin by inviting him to take unconditional permission to go on living. As he lets go of his belief I Mustn't Exist, he will have less and less need for the other belief that he has been using as a defence. Thus he is likely to find he can now cut back his workload relatively easily, and with less impulse to 'sabotage'.

I said that this is 'ideally' the best sequence in which to address compound decisions. There is often a complication in practice, however. When you are making your initial analysis of the client's Racket System, you may not be able to tell immediately whether a particular script decision is acting as a defence against another. You may learn this only after you begin change work with the client, when you notice that he is 'sabotaging' or 'resisting' a particular change. In that case you may look again at your initial picture of his Racket System and consider the possibility that you have missed a compound belief or are addressing one in the wrong order.

One useful fact is that counterscript beliefs will always be used as defence against beliefs from the script proper, never the other way round. Thus whenever your client's presenting problem seems obviously to be connected with a counterscript belief, it is a good idea to consider whether the client may have been using that belief to defend against a potentially more destructive belief from the script proper. If there is a possibility of this being so, plan your treatment so that the client defuses the more destructive belief first.

Compound beliefs and tragic script outcomes

There is one universal principle governing the sequence in which script beliefs should be addressed. It is:

- Always set up protection against tragic script outcomes *before* you invite the client to change any other part of the script.

As I have explained, you can never be certain before you begin change work whether or not a particular script belief is being used as a defence against another, more destructive belief. This may only emerge when the client lets go of one belief and uncovers the other belief against which he has been defending.

But what if the belief thus uncovered is I Mustn't Exist? Admittedly the outcome will most often be simply that your client 'resists' or 'sabotages' some other change. But there is always the chance that he will take his earlier childhood option, and kill or physically harm himself. Alternatively he may translate his early decision into the terms of the other two tragic script outcomes, and either kill or harm someone else or go crazy.

With these possibilities at stake, you clearly cannot go ahead on the basis of trial and error. Instead, you have to ensure that your client has taken secure protection against the three tragic script outcomes before you invite him to make any other change in the script.

John: Compound Decisions and Treatment Direction

The keystone of John's script was the belief 'I Mustn't Exist', arrived at in his early childhood as a response to the destructive messages he had received from his father. In my judgement, John had defended against I Mustn't Exist by combining it with another of the beliefs in his script proper, I Mustn't Be Close. The compound belief ran: 'It's OK for me not to drop dead, so long as I don't ever get close to anybody.'

Knowing the dynamics of the script, I was clear that head-on confrontation of I Mustn't Be Close would most likely result simply in 'resistance' or 'sabotage' on John's part. If John was to take permission to get close to people, he first needed to give himself protection from his lethal early decision I Mustn't Exist.

How can you invite your client to take this protection against tragic outcomes, so crucial to lasting script change? In the coming chapter we look at how this can be done.

Further Reading in *Developing TA Counselling*

Point 6 in *Developing TA Counselling* (Stewart, 1996a) describes an alternative way of gathering script information, using a script questionnaire.

7

BLOCKING TRAGIC OUTCOMES

Closing the Escape Hatches
Further Reading in *Developing TA Counselling*

You will recall from Chapter 3 that there are three tragic script outcomes. They are:

- killing or harming self
- killing or harming others
- going crazy.

Most transactional analysts take the view that to achieve lasting change, one of the most important steps the client can take is to renounce all three of these tragic outcomes.

Closing the Escape Hatches

TA holds that it is possible to renounce these tragic options once and for all. This can be accomplished by a procedure known in TA as 'closing the escape hatches'. The client decides and declares that she will never, under any circumstances, kill or harm herself, kill or harm others, or go crazy.

Crucially, this statement does *not* constitute a *promise* to the counsellor. It is a *decision* made by the client by herself, for herself. Your role is to act as witness. You also watch for any incongruity the client may show when stating her decision.

Clients may be sceptical at first about their ability to make this undertaking firmly and for always. But experience confirms that people who make this decision can and do hold to it.

Closing Escape Hatches as a Basis for Script Change

Why should closing escape hatches be central to script change? Boyd and Cowles-Boyd (1980: 227) explain it as follows:

> The Child thinking usually associated with escape hatches takes the form 'if things get bad enough, I can always (kill myself, kill someone else/them, go crazy)'. No matter how extreme these three tragic options may seem, they are experienced by the Child ... as ultimate solutions to intolerable situations. Patients with escape hatches open are committed to maintaining a reservoir of bad feelings in order to keep the tragic script option available, thus making ... change-oriented contracts unworkable.

The option of killing self is seen as the most fundamental escape hatch. The other two escape hatches act as alternatives to suicide. The child may decide 'I'll kill someone else instead of killing myself.' For go-crazy the decision is: 'Instead of ceasing to exist altogether, I'll cease to exist as a thinking person' (Mellor, 1979).

In closing the escape hatches, the client makes a commitment *from Adult* to renounce all three tragic options. Thus she accepts she is responsible for her own situation. She acknowledges she has power to alter that situation. She becomes free to experience and own a full range of feeling responses without fear of losing control.

She no longer needs to maintain a store of bad feelings that she can use to 'justify' her tragic script payoff. Thus she can also stop setting up the painful situations from which she had gathered those feelings.

The energy she was previously using to maintain her bad feelings now becomes available for other uses. If she wishes, she can employ it to achieve change in the course of counselling.

Escape Hatches and Ego-states

In closing escape hatches, the client asserts her grown-up power to control her own actions. That is, she takes the decision from Adult. The escape-hatch procedure is not intended to address any Child issues she may still have around the tragic options. Her decision then takes the form 'I will not in any circumstances kill or harm self or others nor go crazy, *no matter how bad I may feel.*'

However, experience suggests that the Child ego-state in the client 'hears' the unconditional Adult commitment. This happens in the manner of an internal dialogue. What does escape-hatch closure mean to the Child?

Suddenly, these 'ultimate solutions to intolerable situations' are no longer available. The result often is that the entire structure of the script begins to be dismantled. It is as though closing the escape hatches has pulled out the central pin that held the whole script structure together. The person is deprived of the last-resort solution which she has kept available throughout life to justify the familiar pattern of scripty feelings, thoughts and behaviours. From Child she asks 'So what do I do *now* instead of all that?'

This reassessment takes place largely outside of awareness. For some clients, it may occur gradually. For others, closure of the escape hatches may be followed immediately by a Child response to the new Adult commitment. And this response is often one of panic rather than pleasure. Recall that to the client in Child, the escape hatches have represented ultimate solutions held in reserve for use if things ever get bad enough. Now, suddenly, these ways out are blocked.

This may be reflected in feelings of physical disorientation immediately upon the closure of escape hatches. The client may report a general sense of 'feeling funny' or 'spaced-out'. He may feel a specific emotion that seems inappropriate to the Adult sense of what he has just accomplished. When John finally closed the escape hatches, he morosely complained to me 'But this means I've just lost my comfortable way out!' His 'comfortable way out' had been to punch his hand against solid doors. With some clients, the reaction from Child may not emerge straight away. Instead it becomes evident over a period of days or weeks following the closure of escape hatches. During this time, the client may feel he is 'getting worse instead of better'. Feelings of panic, physical pains and aches, sleep disturbance or depression may all be experienced (Cowles-Boyd, 1980). In this event, you have the option of reassuring the client that their increased discomfort is a sign of positive change.

As time passes, the person adjusts in Child to the new situation. The initial panic reaction gives way to a phase in which he finds Child answers to the question 'What do I do now the escape hatches aren't available?' He begins to realize *in Child* that he no longer needs to store up bad feelings to 'justify' one day going through an escape hatch. Thus he also has less Child motivation to engage in the painful patterns that were used to generate those bad feelings.

Thus when someone closes escape hatches, he may find he begins changing his behaviour in constructive ways, even without conscious intent. This process can be given more direction by contractual work in counselling.

By contrast, what happens if counselling goes ahead while one or more of the client's escape hatches remain open? It is likely that the client will covertly 'sabotage' his stated contract goals. In reality, what is going on below the client's awareness is not 'sabotage'. In Child, it appears the exact opposite. The person is still clinging to the possibility that one day, if things get bad enough, she may go through an escape hatch. And so long as she clings to that option she will also cling to the familiar patterns she has used to 'justify' the options of killing or harming self or others or going crazy.

Closing Escape Hatches as Protection

Closing escape hatches also serves as a physical safeguard against the possibility that the client will actually kill or harm self or others or go crazy. Experience shows that the decision to close escape hatches, *if taken congruently from Adult*, does effectively guard against the three tragic outcomes (Drye, 2006; Drye et al., 1973). Thus by facilitating the client to close the hatches, you provide a central element of *protection* (recall Chapter 1).

Suppose the client is not willing to close one or more of the escape hatches? This warns both of you that she is still holding open one of these 'ultimate ways out'. If this is so, you need to extend temporary protection until she does close the escape hatches. I describe how to do this in a later section.

What if the client agrees overtly to close the escape hatches, but signals some Child reservation in the form of incongruity? Then you need to treat this as if it were an overt refusal to close the hatches.

Closing Escape Hatches as Part of the Treatment Sequence

Boyd and Cowles-Boyd (1980) suggest that:

> the escape hatches should be closed routinely with *all* patients as early in the course of treatment as possible, and without waiting for diagnostic confirmation of the existence of hamartic script outcomes. (Italics in original) *(Note:'hamartic' here means the same as 'tragic')*

It is most important to be clear about what the Boyds are suggesting here, particularly as regards their use of the terms 'routinely' and 'as early as possible':

- *'Routinely'* When the Boyds recommend that you invite escape-hatch closure 'routinely', they mean that you should ask every client to close escape hatches *as standard practice*, whether or not the client brings a presenting problem of self-harm, harming others or going crazy. They absolutely do *not* mean that escape-hatch closure can ever be a matter of 'mere routine', or that it can ever be done 'by rote'. On the contrary, the process of closing escape hatches is a crucial element in change for many clients. It will always call for the full application of your professional skill and judgement.
- *'As early as possible'* In suggesting that you should invite escape-hatch closure 'as early as possible' in treatment, the Boyds mean that you should do so as early in counselling as it is possible for *that individual client* to carry the process through from Adult, with full congruence. They most certainly do *not* mean that you should invite every client to close the hatches in the first session or the first few sessions. There are a minority of clients who may indeed be able to close escape hatches congruently after only a few sessions, but for other clients, it may be months or years before they can get to this point.

Admittedly, some people never made the early decision to open any of the three hatches. Other people may have had them open, but have closed them on their own initiative before coming to counselling. To invite such clients to close escape hatches will do no harm. The client will simply sail through the procedure, taking the Adult decision congruently and easily.

More often, the person will have one or more hatches open. On the surface, this client's problem may appear to have nothing to do with suicide, homicide or going crazy. Nevertheless, he is likely to have been setting up problems for himself because he is unawarely holding open one of the escape hatches. It might take many sessions before you and the client could establish what hatch or hatches the client has been holding open, and what his Child motivation has been for doing so. Instead of waiting that long, you can simply invite him to close all the hatches by Adult decision. This allows him to move more easily and safely to contractual change, for all the reasons I described at the beginning of this chapter.

If the client is not ready to close all three escape hatches, then that becomes the priority for attention, whatever the presenting problem.

How Soon Do You Invite Hatch Closure?

Given that it is not a good idea to invite escape-hatch closure in the first session or first few sessions of counselling, then how soon *should* you invite it? There is no 'copybook' answer to this question, but here are some practical suggestions.

From our discussion of treatment planning in Chapter 2 (Figure 2.2), you have already seen that before raising the question of escape-hatch closure with your client you will usually have completed several of the initial stages of treatment: namely, initial contact, intake, negotiation of the business contract, and diagnosis and assessment. In practice, these steps are likely to take at least four sessions, usually more. You may well then move on to further exploratory work with the client (problem formulation), taking several further sessions. Also, in advance of starting active work in script change, you and the client will spend some time working out the detail of the treatment contract (see Chapter 8).

I suggest, as a pragmatic and flexible rule of guidance, that you might typically consider *raising the topic* of escape-hatch closure with your client between about the fifth and the tenth session. This would therefore usually coincide with problem formulation or the earlier stages of contract-making. If we take 'session number' out of the equation, and think instead about the relationship between you and your client, then you might wait to raise the topic of hatch closure until you have a sense (in Adult and Child) that the client has settled into the counselling process, is getting to know you, and is showing active motivation to change.

By 'raise the topic' I mean that you can explain to your client the purposes of closing escape hatches, and describe the process by which she can close the hatches if she decides to. Whether you then move immediately to *inviting* hatch closure is a matter for your Adult judgement and Child intuition, based on the verbal and non-verbal responses you get back from your client. Sometimes it is a good idea to let the client 'sit with' the idea of closing the hatches for a few sessions, then come round to raising the topic again before moving to invite closure.

And once you have invited the client to close the hatches, how long will he take to do so? The answer is 'As long as it takes.' For you as counsellor, my best advice is: never rush, never push. At the same time, beware of the temptation to bypass the question of hatch closure and instead 'get into the work'. Until the client has congruently closed the hatches, escape hatch closure *is* 'the work'.

With Whom Would You Not Invite Escape-Hatch Closure?

The question here is, 'Are there any circumstances in which you would move into script-change work with a client *without* first inviting her to close escape hatches?'

As you saw from the quotation above, the answer suggested by Boyd and Cowles-Boyd in their influential article (1980) is a simple 'No'. Their stance is that we should invite escape-hatch closure with all clients. And I agree with the Boyds to this extent: you will *never* do any harm to the client by raising the topic of escape-hatch closure, or by inviting the client to close the hatches. This idea often astonishes colleagues from fields other than TA ('You mean to say you actually raise the topic of *suicide,* when the client hasn't been talking about it? But surely that puts the idea of suicide into their mind?'). When we think of the three tragic outcomes in terms of script theory, we realize that if a person already has in their script the belief 'I Mustn't Exist' – as the great majority of people do – then talking about it cannot 'give' them that belief; instead, it brings their existing belief into their Adult awareness, and thus makes it easier for them to begin changing it.

In recent years, there has been a revival of discussion and controversy within TA about the use of escape-hatch closure as a therapeutic procedure. Some transactional analysts suggest that the question of escape hatches is best regarded as part of a wider issue, namely risk assessment and management. If you would like to explore this line of thought, a good overview is given by Mothersole (2006); for recent contributions to the escape-hatch debate, see Boliston-Mardula (2001); Stewart (2001); and Drye (2006). This entire area is still controversial, and transactional analysts are still a long way from general agreement. Pending such agreement – if we ever reach it – my best advice to you is: 'If in doubt, err on the safe side.'

What that means in practice, I suggest, is: If you are seriously considering doing script-change work with a client without inviting escape-hatch closure, be sure to take the case to detailed supervision. That supervision is likely to focus especially on two areas:

1   *Protection:*   as we have seen, closure of escape hatches is designed as an important measure of protection for the client. It is an ethical and professional imperative for transactional analysts to work in such a way as to afford the client the maximum practicable protection at all times. Therefore, if you decide to go ahead with change work in the absence of escape-hatch closure, the question you will always have to address is: How else are you going to extend protection to the client?

One way of doing this is to work within a protected environment, where physical protection against hamartic outcomes is always immediately available. This way of working is well-documented in TA. For example, redecision therapists may work in a 'marathon' setting (that is, a group therapy experience lasting several days or sometimes weeks), where the clients contract to stay within the premises for the entire duration of the marathon (Goulding and Goulding, 1979: 7, 215–40). Cathexis work is often done within residential communities, where continual surveillance by staff and group members can be provided (Schiff et al., 1975).

If you are not working within this kind of protected setting, then, without escape-hatch closure, the provision of physical protection must become a major problem. My own stance as a supervisor is that I will not allow a supervisee to go ahead with script-change work in the absence of hatch closure, unless I am sure that he or she is working within a protected setting.

2   *Availability of Adult:*   we have also seen that closure of escape hatches is done exclusively from an *Adult* ego-state. It follows that if someone does not have reliable access to their Adult functioning, the escape-hatch procedure is likely to be ineffective (or, at the very least, that you as counsellor can never be clear in advance how effective it will be). This means in practice that you will usually not employ the standard escape-hatch procedure with clients who have significant organic brain damage, are actively psychotic, or who are currently abusing substances (for a discussion of work with the last-named client group, see Boliston-Mardula, 2001). And that brings you back to the question we have just been considering: Given that you do not invite hatch closure, how else are you going to maximize the client's protection?

More subtly, there are some clients with personality structures such that although they have access to Adult, they are unlikely to employ Adult to any significant degree while interacting with you – *until* they have completed a substantial amount of script change. We are referring here to clients who would be psychiatrically diagnosable as showing a personality disorder (American Psychiatric Association, 2000: 685–729). In my experience, the disorders most often in the picture here are the Borderline, Narcissistic and Dependent disorders. With such clients, you are in a double-bind: they are most unlikely to close escape hatches congruently until they have made changes in their script; but if you invite these changes without hatch closure, there is a potential risk that the client may actually go through an escape hatch.

A detailed discussion of work with such clients is beyond the scope of this introductory text. As ever, competent supervision is the key. And I would suggest: any time you ask yourself the question 'Will I work with this client without inviting escape-hatch closure?', a prior question to resolve is 'Should I be working with this client at all?'

Escape-hatch Closure for the Counsellor

To be effective in facilitating your clients to close escape hatches, you must have closed them yourself.

If you yourself have one or more of the hatches open, you will be unable to be congruent when you invite the client to close them. You probably have not the slightest intention of committing suicide, harming anyone else or going crazy. Still you need to take time as client with another practitioner to go through the procedure for closing the hatches. You must close them before you carry out the procedure with your own clients.

The Procedure for Closing Escape Hatches

In the remainder of this chapter, I shall refer to my work with John to illustrate the procedure of closing escape hatches. He took a long time to make the decision. I raised the issue with him in our fifth session; it was not until session eleven that John finally closed all his escape hatches congruently. Once he had done so, he was quick to achieve further script change.

Key Ideas 7.1

CLOSING ESCAPE HATCHES

1   'Closing escape hatches' means that the client decides and declares that she will never, under any circumstances, kill or harm herself, kill or harm anyone else, or go crazy.

2   The client makes this decision for herself, with the counsellor acting as witness; the client is *not* making a 'promise' to the counsellor.

3   The decision to close the escape hatches is made in the Adult ego state, not in Child or Parent.

4   For effective closure of escape hatches, the procedure can never be done 'by rote'. It requires you to exercise all your professional skill and judgement in assessing the client's congruence. It requires the client to be at a point in counselling where he is ready to make the hatch-closure decision with full intent.

5   To close escape hatches, the client's autonomous undertaking not to kill or harm self or others or go crazy must be *permanent and unconditional*. The client commits herself congruently to keep the hatches closed for the remainder of her natural life, no matter what may happen. Anything less means the hatches are not fully closed.

6   All three escape hatches should be addressed at one time. If the client has more than one hatch open, closure of one may increase the likelihood that she will exercise another or others.

7   During the process of closing escape hatches, both client and counsellor must operate at all times from an Adult ego-state. If you detect any hint of incongruity, it is best to assume the hatch has not been closed.

Closure of the escape hatches is a *decision*, not a *contract* (Drye, 2006). A contract can be reviewed, renegotiated and changed if client and counsellor so agree. By contrast, the essence of closing escape hatches is that the client's decision is irrevocable and non-negotiable.

Wording

The procedure I followed with John is typical of TA practice. First, I explained to him what the three-part decision entailed. I said:

> There's a procedure in TA that we call 'closing the escape hatches'. I believe it's an essential step to take if you want to make lasting changes in yourself. To close the escape hatches, you would decide never, under any circumstances, to kill or harm yourself, kill or harm anybody else, or go crazy.

If you do go ahead and make these decisions, they'll be decisions you make for you. They will *not* be promises you make to me. My job is to act as witness to the decisions you make. I'll also reflect back to you whether I think you're making them from your clear Adult self, or whether I think you may be giving yourself some Child let-outs without knowing it.

If you do make these decisions, they will be for always, and they'll be unconditional. You'll be deciding never to take any of these options, no matter what may happen and no matter how you feel. So you may want to think about it for a bit. Do you want to go ahead now and close these escape hatches?

As many clients do, John opened a discussion about whether it was possible for him to make these decisions permanently and unconditionally. Some of this was from Adult. But it also reflected a Child doubt whether he was able to take responsibility for his own actions and thinking. My response was to convey the information that, yes, people can make these decisions for always and without reservation. I told John that I had known many people who had made these decisions and stuck to them. I added that I had closed the escape hatches myself. Therefore, I could personally confirm that it was possible to keep them closed permanently and unconditionally.

John still had doubts, and I knew it was important to stay with these until they had been fully resolved. Whatever the presenting problem may be, the issue to be tackled at this point is the client's ability to take responsibility for his own conduct and thinking. In particular, he needs to confirm that he can control his own impulses toward self-harm, harming others or abandoning his sanity. For some clients, like John, this may take many sessions, and may constitute the main therapeutic work that the client will do in counselling.

In our eleventh session, John finally said he was ready to close all the hatches. I then outlined to him the way to signal his decision:

OK, if you go ahead now and close the hatches, you can do it by taking the following decisions for yourself:

- That you will never, in any circumstances, kill or harm yourself, try to kill or harm yourself, or set up to kill or harm yourself, accidentally or on purpose.
- That you will never, in any circumstances, kill or harm anyone else, try to kill or harm anyone else, or set up to kill or harm anyone else, accidentally or on purpose.

- That you will never, in any circumstances, go crazy, try to go crazy, or set up to go crazy, accidentally or on purpose.

You can use different words if you want. Closing escape hatches means saying clearly you are making these decisions for always and no matter what may happen. Please, only say these things if you can say them and mean them. So, if you are willing to, go ahead and make these decisions now.

Checking for incongruity

Throughout the procedure for closing escape hatches, you must monitor your own and your client's ego-states. In particular, it is important that you stay alert for incongruities that signal your client may have shifted into Child. If so, his undertaking is likely to be a promise to you instead of a decision for himself. Like all promises, such a one is 'made to be broken'.

Incongruity may take the form of a non-verbal signal. For instance, the client may put his hand over his mouth. He may chuckle or grimace or shake his head. Whenever you detect any hint of incongruity, assume that the client is discounting his statement. You might confront by saying: 'When you were making the statement about never killing or harming others, you held your hand in front of your mouth. Will you take your hand away from your mouth? Now will you find out if you're willing to make the statement and mean it?'

You may also hear verbal disclaimers, such as:

'I *would* never kill myself.'
'I don't have the courage to kill myself.'
'I'd *never want to* harm anyone else.'

In all these cases too, you must address what the client is really saying. None of these statements is the same as a firm undertaking 'I *will* never ... '. Your task is to be aware of the ulterior messages your client is conveying. Each time he does this, you should draw the possible let-out to his attention and ask if he is willing to make the statement, and mean it, without the let-out. If he is not, resist the temptation to 'railroad' him or pretend that the let-out is not there. Instead, call a halt after a reasonable time. Tell your client that it seems to you he isn't yet ready to close that hatch unconditionally. You and he can then begin to explore what he is setting up for himself by not closing the hatch. First, however, you need to set up temporary protection. I describe how to do this in a later section.

You must also monitor *yourself* for incongruity during the procedure. Be alert in particular for any sign that you are slipping into Parent. Any hint from you of 'I'd like you to ...' or 'Can you ...?' or 'Here's what you have to do ...', and the client's response is most likely to take the form of a Child 'promise'.

Exceptions

Some clients will say they are willing to close a particular hatch, but only with specified exceptions. Examples:

'I will never kill myself. Well, except if I get very ill when I'm old and am in great pain or become a vegetable.'
'I'll never commit suicide in the normal way of things. But if there's a nuclear war and everybody is dying of radiation, then I'd want to put myself out of my misery.'
'Of course I'll never harm or kill anyone else. Except maybe if I were to see a grown-up man beating a child. Then I'd feel I was justified in attacking him.'
'I'd only kill someone if they were going to kill me.'

You should regard any such exception as if it were an outright refusal to close the hatch. No matter how reasonable an exception may seem on the social level, its ulterior Child purpose may be to leave open the tragic script ending which may some day be invoked 'if things just get bad enough'. The worst-case scenario pictured by the client usually has more to do with scary Child fantasies than with anything that is likely to happen in the real future. If you explore the suggested exceptions, they may lead you and your client into fruitful areas of insight. It is often useful to pose an Adult question about the scope of the exception. Examples:

'Tell me what would have to happen so that you knew nuclear war had been declared. Would somebody actually have to have dropped a nuclear bomb somewhere?'
'What would somebody have to do so you knew without doubt that they meant to kill you?'
'So you'd attack somebody if they were attacking another person. It sounds to me like you want to take over the job of the police. Do you?'

In reality, closing the escape hatches does mean giving up certain options for which there may be some Adult rationale. An example might be euthanasia in the case of terminal illness. By closing the suicide escape hatch, the person voluntarily forgoes this choice. He has to balance this potential loss against the benefits he will derive from closing the escape hatches unconditionally.

Accidents

Sometimes the client will propose a similar let-out by suggesting he may go through one of the escape hatches accidentally. Example:

> 'I'll never kill myself on purpose. But of course I can't guarantee not to have an accident in the car some time, with the roads like they are these days.'

You may respond to this by asking:

> 'Do you mean that when you drive your car, you don't have control of it?'

Usually the client will reply that he has. With that reply he may gain insight into the nature of his Child let-out. If the client congruently replies that he does *not* have full control of his car, then you both become aware of a priority objective in counselling! The phrase 'accidentally or on purpose' in the escape-hatch procedure is designed to guard against 'accidents' which the client may set up without awareness.

Of course, there are genuine accidents on the road and elsewhere. But this is irrelevant to escape-hatch closure. If the client is struck by lightning, a runaway truck or a falling roof-tile while behaving in a manner that in no way sets up for these outcomes, then he is not harming self. He is being harmed.

The meaning of 'go crazy'

Often a client will ask: 'What do you mean by "go crazy"?'

You may respond by asking in turn: 'Well, what do you mean by it?'

In any case it is useful to raise this question yourself before the client goes on to close the escape hatches. Sometimes the client will reveal that he equates the notion of 'going crazy' with letting go of control. This may not correspond to a majority view of 'craziness':

> 'Well, going crazy to me would be losing control of my feelings – flailing around, getting red in the face, screaming at people.'

You can then discuss this interpretation with the client. For the purposes of closing escape hatches, 'going crazy' means any kind of thinking or behaviour that would be likely to attract the clinical diagnosis of 'psychotic'.

The client on medication

Special considerations arise if your client is taking minor tranquillizers or anti-depressants at the time he closes escape hatches. The effect of these medications is to blank off the agitation, anxiety or depression that the person has been feeling. In ego-state terms, part of the Child or Parent ego-state is decommissioned, temporarily taking the sting out of whatever unfinished script issues were at the root of the person's discomfort. However, when the client cuts down or discontinues the medication, these issues and the feelings that go with them are reactivated.

Thus when a client is on medication it is possible for her to close escape hatches *congruently*, yet still re-open them if she reduces or ceases the medication. This is the only circumstance in which congruent closure can be unreliable.

If your client does close escape hatches while on medication, your best course is to explain to her that the drugs are shutting down a part of her that might possibly want to reconsider the decision. So long as she continues on the same level of medication, you can proceed as though she had the hatches closed. But as soon as she begins reducing dosage, you must repeat the procedure for closing the hatches, watching for incongruity just as closely as you did originally. You may have to repeat this several times until the client has ceased the medication and is well clear of its effects.

If the Client Does Not Close Escape Hatches

What if the client does not close all the escape hatches during a session? You *must* then follow a further procedure designed to monitor the degree of risk and give temporary protection. This must be done before the client leaves your presence. You must therefore keep time in reserve as necessary towards the close of the session. The guidelines to follow are:

- If the client will not close escape hatches, you must agree temporary closure before the session ends.
- You must check again before the temporary closure runs out, and extend the period if necessary.

Suppose that, after a reasonable amount of discussion, your client still is not willing to say congruently that he will never commit suicide or harm himself. You must then continue by enquiring for how long he is willing to refrain from going through the hatch:

> I hear that you're not willing to say now that you'll never, in any circumstances, kill or harm yourself. So what I'm asking you now instead is *how long* you're willing to make that undertaking for? Maybe until our next session? Or maybe you'll make that decision for the next month? Maybe for some other length of time? So, for how long will you undertake for certain not to kill or harm yourself?

Your client may congruently reply 'Until our next session.' If so, you must raise the matter again at that next session without fail. You must ask again whether the client is ready to close the hatch permanently. If he is not, then you must repeat the procedure of time-limited closure.

If he undertakes to keep the hatches closed for some other period, then you must re-check with your client before that period is up.

In my work with John, I carried through this procedure of time-limited closure throughout the period between our fifth and eleventh sessions. In the first two of these weeks, the closure was from one session to the next. Subsequently John undertook to keep the hatches closed for two-week periods, until his eventual unconditional closure. I believe that time-limited closure of this kind provides experiential learning for the person in Child, giving 'practice' at keeping the hatches closed.

Time-limited closure, *so long as it is congruent,* is a great asset to the treatment process because of the following fact: while you are working within the agreed time limit, you can safely move with the client to active script change. To put it another way: during congruent time-limited closure of the hatches, you can undertake any therapeutic move that you could undertake if there were full closure. It is your responsibility, not the client's, then to keep track of the time-limit and to invite the client to extend the period of closure *before* the time-limit runs out.

Escape-hatch emergencies

It is seldom that a client will refuse to close an escape hatch until at least your next session. But if this does happen, what do you do? Realize that a client in this position is telling you explicitly that he may, before he sees you again, kill himself, kill someone else or go crazy. These extreme possibilities call for extreme responses from you. You must go on to ask the client how long, then, he *is* willing to refrain from any of these options. If he says, for example, 'twenty-four hours', then you must fix to see him again before that time is up. At that session in turn you must check how long he is willing to keep the hatches closed.

Suppose your client is not willing to close an escape hatch even for a short period? You must then arrange alternative protection straight away. You must do this before the client leaves your presence. The tactic of choice is to arrange for the client to enter hospital. For counsellors in the UK working outside medical or some social-work settings, this course is not open. Instead, you must contact the client's GP immediately and inform him or her of the position. Recall from Chapter 5 that at intake you reserved the right to break confidentiality in just this circumstance.

When the Client Does Close the Hatches

When John made his clear Adult statement to close each escape hatch, I carried out one further step. Staying in Adult myself, I asked: 'Is that statement true for you?'

Observing how he answered, I made a final check for any hint of incongruity. I repeated the question for each of the three escape hatches separately.

When I was sure John had closed all the hatches congruently, I congratulated him on the important change he had achieved for himself.

Self-supervision 7.1

CLOSING ESCAPE HATCHES

Before inviting your clients to close escape hatches, book time with a counsellor or therapist and close the escape hatches for yourself.

When you have accomplished this, invite your chosen client to close the escape hatches. If she is not willing to do so immediately, carry through the procedure for time-limited closure.

(Continued)

(Continued)

When your client is ready, complete the procedure for closing the hatches. Listen to the tape of this session, checking for incongruities. Be alert for incongruities on *your* part as well as the client's. If you detect that you missed some incongruity during the session, re-open the issue with your client and re-run the procedure until you are confident she has closed the escape hatches congruently.

With the escape hatches closed, your client now has a firm foundation for change. The next step is to work out a specific outcome for change and negotiate what you and your client will do to bring about that outcome. This is the process of *contract-making*, discussed in the coming chapter.

Further Reading in *Developing TA Counselling*

Point 7 in *Developing TA Counselling* (Stewart, 1996a) gives some further guidelines on inviting your client to close escape hatches. I stress there that the procedure must always be treated as a major move in therapy, and that escape-hatch closure can never be set as a 'rule'.

8

MAKING CONTRACTS FOR CHANGE

The Meaning of 'Contractual Method'
Effective Contract-making
Contract-making and Treatment Direction
Dealing With 'Sabotage'
Further Reading in *Developing TA Counselling*

Eric Berne (1966: 362) defined a *contract* as 'an explicit bilateral commitment to a well-defined course of action.' When you and your client make a contract in TA work, you agree between you a clear statement of the change the client is going to make. You specify also what each of you is going to contribute to the achievement of that change.

In some other counselling approaches, the word 'contract' is used in a more restricted sense, meaning an agreement about the number of sessions the client and counsellor are going to spend together. In TA usage, this is only one of several points that will be specified in the contract (Sills, 2006; Stewart, 1996a, 2006).

Early in the counselling relationship, you and your client agreed upon your *business contract* (recall Chapter 5). This set out details of payment and administrative matters such as place and frequency of attendance.

Now, with the stage set for change, you go on to formulate a *treatment contract*. The client specifies a personal change that he intends to achieve. You say whether you are willing to work with the client in achieving it. As part of the change process, you may negotiate contracts for specific actions on the part of either client or counsellor.

You will recall from Chapter 5 Steiner's requirement of *mutual consent* for sound contract-making. Where the business contract is concerned, few would doubt the need for mutual consent. However, if you are new to TA work, the idea of mutual consent on the *treatment* contract may seem less obvious to you. You may be familiar with the notion that your client should specify what changes he wants to make. But you may be less used to the suggestion that it is open to *you* to accept or reject these proposed changes as goals you are willing to work for.

In this chapter I begin by reviewing the nature and objectives of contract-making. I go on to describe how you can make an effective treatment contract. Next I discuss ways in which you can plan your contract-making to achieve effective treatment direction. The final section describes how, without awareness, your client may attempt to 'sabotage' contract-making. I explain ways in which you can forestall this.

The Meaning of 'Contractual Method'

Whatever detailed technique you use in contract-making, there are two simple conditions that define contractual method. To check on these you can ask the following questions:

- Have you and your client agreed between you a *definition* of whatever personal change the client intends to make?
- Have you and the client *explicitly* agreed that the client will make that change, and that you will facilitate her in doing so?

If you can answer 'Yes' to both these questions, then you and your client have a contract for change.

Naturally, there will be times during the counselling process during which you and your client are actively engaged in working out the contract. This will almost always be the case during the early stages of counselling, when the client often begins with only a very general idea of what change he wants to achieve. Later in the course of treatment, there are likely to be times when you and your client return to discussing and re-negotiating the contract – either because the client has achieved a contract goal already agreed, or because a new objective has emerged from the client's self-discovery. At such times, although you and the client have not yet agreed a specific contract, you are still 'working contractually': the focus of your work is on making that contract.

From session to session and from moment to moment, you may suggest to your client that he do specific things in furtherance of his overall goal. His side of the contract then is to say explicitly whether or not he is willing to follow this course of action. Likewise, he may ask specific actions of you, and it is open to you to signify if you are willing to do what he asks.

All formal techniques of contract-making are frameworks to help assure that these conditions are met. In practical counselling, the first and most important task is usually to arrive at a clearly agreed definition of the change the client wants to make.

The Timing of the Treatment Contract

Some general books on counselling and psychotherapy have suggested that in TA practice, a specific treatment contract is always determined in the first few sessions (I have even seen it suggested that 'the contract is always made in the first session'). This is a misapprehension. The reality is that some clients, indeed, are ready to agree a clear contract for change at a relatively early stage in counselling. With other clients, it may take weeks or months of painstaking work in counselling before the client is in a place where she is ready to work out a specific contract. Indeed, with such clients, the clear elicitation of the treatment contract may itself be the crucial move in personal change.

The Purposes of Contract-making

Why do transactional analysts put so much emphasis on using contracts?

One reason lies in TA's philosophical stance that 'people are OK'. Client and counsellor are neither one-up nor one-down to each other. It is assumed also that each person is responsible for his own decisions and actions. From this it follows that you and your client take joint responsibility for the process of change. If that responsibility is to mean anything, both of you need to understand and agree upon what you are there to do.

The use of contracts also brings several practical advantages:

1   *The client is actively involved in the counselling process.*   She engages her own motivation to change right from an early stage of the counselling process. She need never feel she is being passively 'done to'.

What is more, *you* are relieved of any feeling that it is up to you to decide how the client 'should' change. Without a contract, you end up with a double responsibility: you are expected to decide not only *how* the client can be helped to change, but also *what* it is she should be changing. In contractual work, you only have the first half of this responsibility. I experience this as one of the greatest benefits of working contractually.

2   *The contract provides a mental set towards change.* In agreeing a goal
for change, both you and your client have to construct a mental image of
that goal. For reasons that are still not well understood, this positive visualization seems to empower achievement of the outcome. To realize this
advantage fully, you need to pay careful attention to the wording of the
contract. I shall explain this in more detail in a later section.

3   *Counsellor and client know clearly when their work together is complete.* The contract is a clear statement of a goal. Therefore both you
and your client can tell without doubt whether that goal has been
achieved. This guards against the possibility that the counselling relationship may drag on for months or years without any clear end-point.

4   *Contract-making guards against imposition of the counsellor's goals on the
client.* Every counsellor has her own ideas about how people should be.
Without a contract, there is always the possibility that you may unknowingly seek to influence your client into making the changes you feel he
should make, rather than the changes he wants to make.

At the same time, your own goals and ideals for personal change do
figure in the negotiation of the contract. For instance, if someone
came to me asking for counselling to enable him to become better at
selling people goods they didn't really want, I would decline that
contract because I am not comfortable with its objective.

5   *The contract discourages pursuit of covert agendas.* This point follows
closely on the last. Both you and your client come to your relationship
with preconceived notions about what you are there to achieve. Some
of these preconceptions may be overt, as for instance my unwillingness to work with the would-be salesman. But others may be covert.
This will seldom be a matter of either yourself or your client know-
ingly setting out to deceive the other. Rather, both of you are likely to
have some attitudes that are not fully in your own awareness. As counsellor you may, without knowing it, be making judgements like:

> 'This client can't get by without my help.'
> 'This person doesn't need help – he should just pull himself
> together.'
> 'I know what this client needs without his telling me.'

And your client may be making his own self-statements outside of
awareness:

> 'I can't get by without this counsellor's help.'
> 'I've come to change, but I don't have the power to do it.'
> 'I'm damned if this person is going to make me change!'

TA holds that the outcome of communication is always determined by what is going on at the psychological and not the social level (recall Chapter 1). Therefore, unless you and your client lay bare the 'secret messages' you are conveying to each other, you are likely to devote your energies to pursuing these covert aims. One function of contract-making is to bring the secret messages out into the open.

It is likely that neither you nor your client will succeed in bringing to light your entire covert agenda at the beginning of your relationship. Therefore it is usual to review your contract at frequent intervals during counselling.

Effective Contract-making

The treatment contract, like the business contract, must meet Steiner's four requirements (see Chapter 5). Once you have assured this, you can go on to consider six questions:

1   Is the contract goal feasible?
2   Is it safe?
3   Is it stated in positive words?
4   Is it observable?
5   Is it placed in a clear context?
6   Does it mark a movement out of script and into autonomy for the client?

When you can answer 'Yes' to all these questions, you have an effective treatment contract.

Feasibility

The test of feasibility is to check: 'Has at least one other person in the world achieved this?' If the answer is 'Yes', then the contract goal is judged potentially feasible. At the same time, it is necessary to consider carefully what the 'this' entails, taking into account the client's age, current skills and so on. As a general guideline, be optimistic while being realistic.

For a contract to be feasible, it has to speak of a change that the person wants to make in herself. It is not possible to make a feasible contract for change in someone else.

Safety

This implies both physical and legal safety. It may also raise questions of social appropriateness. For instance, suppose a woman client wants to take the contract goal of assertively choosing a man as a marriage partner. In Western social groupings, this is likely to be a safe goal, but among some other cultural groups such action might bring disagreeable or dangerous social consequences for the client.

You know from Chapters 3 and 7 that safety also means *protection* against the possible tragic script outcomes that the client may have been holding in reserve. The main implication for contract-making is that you *must not invite a contract for script change until the client has closed escape hatches.* However, you can take purely exploratory contracts before that point. In exploratory work, you and the client will be discovering how he has been creating and maintaining problems for himself. You will also be considering what he might do differently to achieve the changes he wants. Neither of these things is the same as actually changing.

Positive Wording

Frequently a person comes into counselling with the aim of stopping doing something. She will typically state her initial goal in negative words. She may want to:

- *stop* having fights with her relations
- *give up* smoking
- *not* be nervous of speaking in public
- *control* her emotions
- *lose* weight.

For an effective treatment contract, any such negative goals must be re-phrased in positive words.

Negative contracts are hardly ever effective in the long term. A 'stop contract' like this is likely to mean that the client will set up an internal Parent–Child struggle. She will keep some behaviour painfully under control through the exercise of 'willpower'. Usually in this situation it is only a matter of time before the client runs out of energy to keep the struggle going. When she does, she is likely to be even more ready to indulge the Child urge that she has been controlling. One familiar example is where the person *controls* her diet, *loses* weight, then binges and puts the weight back on again.

There are several reasons why most 'stop contracts' are ineffective. Consider first how the contract statement acts as a visualization. It is impossible to visualize 'not something'. For example, test visualizing 'not a running dog'. When you attempt this, you automatically make a picture of whatever follows the 'not'. Thus if, for instance, someone makes a contract to 'not be afraid', he cannot address this contract goal without continually visualizing 'being afraid'.

Further, a negatively worded contract gives the person no clear directive to what he *is* going to do. It simply adds yet another to the list of 'stops' and 'don'ts' that all of us got from our parents when we were little. As young children, we decided on patterns of behaviour because they seemed to be the best way of getting needs met and surviving. When we replay these strategies as grown-ups, that is still our Child motivation. Therefore if we simply contract to 'stop' or 'control' these behaviours, we may experience this in Child as threatening the satisfaction of our needs or even our survival. Small wonder that we usually find ways of sabotaging this kind of contract.

To be effective in the long term, the contract needs to provide *at least one more option* than the old behaviour. This gives the person a positive course of action that will meet his Child needs at least as effectively as the behaviour he wishes to stop.

Often the negotiation of a positively worded contract can itself be therapeutic. For example, consider what happens when your client suggests the negative contract 'I will stop smoking', and you decline to take on that contract. To move ahead from that point, you might ask your client 'What are you going to do *instead of* smoking that will satisfy the needs you used to satisfy by smoking?'

You and she may take some time to get to a satisfactory answer to that question. But when you do, the client will have the basis for a lasting change without continual 'willpower' struggles.

Observability

An effective treatment contract must specify the contract goal in a way that is *observable*. This is central to contract-making in TA. By 'observable' we mean that the contract should be stated in such a way that you can check its achievement by using any of your five senses (Stewart, 1996a: 78–83). Can you see, hear or physically feel that the contract is being fulfilled? (Smelling or tasting may also be relevant to some contracts.) If yes, the contract is observable. Another way to say this is that the contract is *sensory-based*.

Often, careful attention to the wording of a contract is needed to check whether it is observable. I shall illustrate this by an example from my work with John.

John: Making an Observable Contract

When John and I were initially discussing the changes he wanted to make in counselling, he said that one of his goals was 'to get closer to people'.

This statement certainly specified that he wanted to change his way of relating to others. But it was far from being observable. To develop an observable translation of this goal, he and I needed answers to several questions. Our exchange (in session twelve) went as follows:

JOHN: I want to get closer to people. *(Over-generalizes)*
COUNSELLOR: Which people?
JOHN: Oh, people I know well, people I like. *(Still not observable; who, by name?)*
COUNSELLOR: Name one of these people?
JOHN: Well, Helen *(girlfriend)*, certainly.

Now that John and I were talking about a specific person, he and I could go on to work out a description of what he would be doing when he 'got closer to' his girlfriend.

COUNSELLOR: How will you and Helen know that you're getting closer to her in the way you want to?
JOHN: [Pause] Because when she speaks to me, I'll listen to her, instead of just paying attention to myself.

We were now closer to observability, because we were talking about specific ways of relating between these two people. But we had still not determined how John or Helen would know, using any of their senses, whether John was 'listening to her', and whether that was 'instead of paying attention to himself'. So I went on to ask him another question:

COUNSELLOR: How will you and she know you are listening to her instead of paying attention to yourself?
JOHN: [Long pause] Because I'll give her time to speak, and then I'll tell her how I'm feeling about what she's said to me.

COUNSELLOR: Ah, so you and Helen will know you're listening to her when you give her time to speak and then tell her how you're feeling about what she says?

JOHN: Yes.

At this point we had an observable translation of the generalized goal that John had started with. There was still one thing missing. John had begun by saying there was something he 'wanted' to do. If we had left the process there, he would simply have finished up with a more specific want. He had still not said whether he was going to do anything about it. I thus went on:

COUNSELLOR: So, will you do that at least once in the coming week and report back to me when we next meet?

JOHN: [*With congruent Adult body signals*] Yes, I will.

With this, we had an observable contract.

Why observability is important

Why is so much emphasis placed on observability? One reason is that only by this kind of contract can you assess whether the stated goal has been reached. Suppose John and I had contracted for a vague goal like 'getting closer to people'. Neither of us would ever have been able to tell whether he had got sufficiently close to enough people to fulfil the contract.

Further, John and I needed to compare our images of what 'getting close to people' entailed. My own first image of 'getting close' implied physical closeness. To John, as it turned out, 'getting close' meant the intimate sharing of feelings with another person. Without an observable contract, we might have gone ahead believing we were aiming for the same goal when in fact our goals were different.

Recall also how the contract goal acts as a positive visualization. It is well established that the more sensory detail you can put into a visualization, the more effective it will be. If I want to programme myself to achieve a goal, I can do so most powerfully by imagining myself achieving the outcome I desire, with full 'sound and visuals'. I might add details of physical sensations, smells and tastes. In negotiating an observable contract, you and your client carry through just this process.

'Observable' vs. 'behavioural'

In the literature of TA, it has been traditional to demand that any effective contract be *behavioural* – that is, that the contract be for a specific action. Indeed, this is central to Eric Berne's definition of a contract, given above (Berne, 1966: 362). The unspoken assumption has been that in order to be observable, a contract statement must also be behavioural.

In practice, however, the contracts that people agree upon in effective counselling are as often about *outcomes* as they are about actions. Indeed, in my experience, the contracts most crucial to personal change are likely to centre on outcomes rather than on actions. Furthermore, outcomes – as well as actions – can perfectly well be observable. For example:

'I will get a new job paying at least £... per year.'
'I will be living together with a new partner.'
'I will change my body-fat percentage to 15 per cent.'

Each of these statements is sensory-based: it is possible to check on their achievement using sight and hearing, and perhaps other senses also. But none of the statements describe an action; they all describe outcomes. For example, 'getting a new job' is a desired outcome; it says nothing about what the person is going to *do* to achieve that outcome. An outcome describes a state of affairs, while an action describes behaviour.

I have therefore suggested (Stewart, 1996a: 67; 2006: 63–4) that we can usefully employ the terms *outcome contract* and *action contract*, with an 'action contract' corresponding to the traditional 'behavioural contract'. For effective contract-making, both outcome and action contracts need to be sensory-based.

If a contract is for an outcome, then it must be supported by at least one contract for an action. Why? Because only by *doing* something can the person interact with the world. If the person's desired outcome is 'to get a new job', he must carry out at least one action to help bring that outcome about. If he does not act, nothing new will happen. For the person whose outcome contract is to get the new job, some relevant action contracts might be:

'Buy the local paper and read the job adverts.'
'Write up my c.v. and have it printed out by an agency.'
'Read a book about doing job interviews.'

Context

For fully effective contract-making, it is advisable to take account of the *context* of the contract (Stewart, 1996a: 97–102). To determine the context of a contract, you and your client will agree answers to the following three questions:

1   *Where* will the contract be carried out?
2   *When?*
3   Under what *limiting conditions?*

It may seem at first sight as though the issue of context is dealt with by the demand that contracts should be sensory-based. On closer inspection, however, it turns out that this is not necessarily so. Take, for example, a simple behavioural contract like this one: 'In the coming week, I will say hello to three people I haven't spoken to before.'

This statement is clearly sensory-based. However, the contract statement as it stands misses out part of the context. The *time* dimension of the contract is indeed specific ('in the coming week'). This answers the question 'when?' But the dimension of 'where' is left unclear. Will the client say hello to three people on the upper deck of the bus, in the supermarket, at home, or just to three people anywhere?

Further, we do not know from the contract statement whether there are any circumstances in which the client would *not* carry out the contract. These are what I call 'limiting conditions'. For example, if the client is a woman, is she going to 'say hello to a new person' if that person is an unknown man she happens to pass in a deserted city street?

Here are some specific questions that you can ask to elicit the three basic modalities of context: time, place and limiting conditions.

- *Where?*   Where is the client going to do the action contracted for? Is it in some specific setting, for example, at her work, in her home? (A check question here is 'What is the place by name?') Or is it to be in a generic setting, for example, whenever on top of a bus, or at some time when on the street? Or is the contract to apply anywhere and everywhere?
- *When?*   You can investigate the time dimension of context by asking the client questions such as:

  'By what date?'
  'How many weeks, months, years from now?'
  'How often?'
  'How many times?'
  'For how long once you have begun?'

An important aim is to elicit from the client a statement of how long (or how often) the contract statement will need to be put into action for the client to be willing to say: 'Yes, that contract is completed now.' Does she just need to do it once? If several times, how many times? If the focus is on achieving an end-point in a process (such as in a contract for reducing body fat), for how long does the target situation need to be held in place before the client will count the contract goal as having been achieved?

* *Under what limiting conditions?* The 'limiting conditions', of course, are already partly defined by 'where' and 'when'. Also, you will have begun to specify limiting conditions as you worked out with your client with whom specifically he is going to carry out the contract. Will the client carry out the contract when he is with one specific person or one specific group of people, for example, when he is with his children, or when he is with the five people who currently work in the office with him? (Again a check question here is, 'With whom by name?') Or is the contract to be completed with a generically defined group, for example, whenever with any workmates, or whenever he is with any people he has not met before? Or does the client specifically intend carrying out the contract with anyone and everyone? Additional questions that may be useful are:

'What does the other person have to do first?'
'How will you know that it's time for you to do this?'
'Are there any circumstances in which you're not going to do this?'

Beware the 'invisible context'

It is as well to be cautious of agreeing statements of context like the following:

'I'll show my feelings *when it's appropriate to show them.*'
'I'll express anger to my partner *when I feel angry.*'

The common feature of statements like these is that they specify a contextual circumstance that refers only to the client's own internal experience, and not to anything externally observable. I call this an 'invisible context'.

These 'invisible context' statements seem, and sometimes are, expressions of appropriate caution. But in my experience they are more often cop-outs. Outside of awareness, the person is defending against script change. She is likely to discover that the occasion never seems to come when it is 'appropriate' to show her feelings, or that she seems inexplicably to have stopped 'feeling angry' just when she was on the point of expressing anger.

Useful check questions to pick up this kind of 'invisible context' are:

'If I were a fly on the wall, how would I know that the time had come when it was "appropriate" for you to show how you feel?'
'Are you willing to show your anger even if you don't believe you feel it?'

There may be some occasions on which the client will autonomously decide to leave the context unspecified, in whole or in part. In that event, the open context gives the person more flexibility, hence more genuine option, in deciding where, when and with whom to carry out the contract.

Contract-making and Script Change

Though contracts in TA are typically focused on highly specific new outcomes or behaviour, these changes in themselves are seldom the sole purpose of the contract. Most often, the specified change is chosen because it *indicates a movement out of script for the client*. This is why contract-making needs to be guided by a knowledge of your client's script beliefs and other features of the Racket System.

John: Contract-making and Script Change

In the case extract above, John began by saying he wanted to 'get closer to people'. The final observable translation of that goal was that, at least once during the week, he would give his girlfriend time to speak and then tell her how he felt about what she had said.

This observable contract has the various advantages I have just been describing. However, it may seem at first sight to have trivialized the issue that John came with. His stated problem was not whether he could spend some time listening and feeding back to his girlfriend; it was about being close to people.

But when you view the specific contract goal in relation to John's script, you will see that it did address the broader problem. John had had difficulty in 'getting close to people'. This reflected what we had already discovered from compiling his Racket System, namely that 'I Mustn't Be Close' was one of his script beliefs. Now he was contracting for a behaviour that was for him one way of 'getting close to people'. In so doing, he was deliberately acting in a way that challenged his script belief.

This behavioural change was innocuous in the here-and-now, but it had vast implications for John in Child. It meant he was breaking a pattern of behaviour that he had viewed since his early childhood as being essential to his survival.

As it turned out, John reported at each of the next two sessions that he had carried out the behavioural contract. In doing this, he faced up to his scare. He began the process of learning by experience that he *could* survive as a grown-up without using the strategies he had decided upon as an infant. This learning was made in Child as well as in Adult. For John, it marked a movement out of script and into autonomy.

Behaviour as a marker for script change

In my work with clients, I sometimes explain this by saying that the contractually agreed behaviour acts as a *marker* for script change.

The behavioural marker may be something the client is going to do either in a counselling session or outside it. Shortly after John completed the contract I have just been describing, he took another contract for an in-session behaviour: 'I will put my father on another chair in fantasy and I will tell him I'm going to keep on living, no matter what.'

If you agree an out-of-session marker, it is necessary to specify in the contract that the client is going to report to you about it. Otherwise, as far as you are concerned, the contract would not be for an observable behaviour. A similar point applies when the client's desired outcome is to 'feel different' about a particular person or situation. In that case also, your effective response is to invite the client to take a contract to *tell you* when they are feeling different in the way they want. It is the 'telling' that is the behavioural marker.

Contract-making and Treatment Direction

In Chapter 2 you met the 'Treatment Triangle' (Figure 2.1). It showed how there is always a three-way interplay between *contract, diagnosis* and *treatment direction*. The last of these entails deciding what interventions to make, how to make them, and in what order to make them.

At this stage in the treatment sequence you have already collected diagnostic data at intake (Chapter 5) and by compiling the details of your client's Racket System (Chapter 6). You can now relate this knowledge to the other two corners of the Treatment Triangle. In the light of your knowledge of the client's script and her general goals for change, what contracts might you invite her to take that would further her movement out of script? In what order might you invite her to address these contracts? By answering these questions, you will help determine an effective direction for treatment.

As always, the initial version of your treatment plan may be revised as you and your client continue to work together.

In the coming subsection I discuss how you can use your knowledge of script dynamics in deciding treatment direction. I go on to review some practical aspects of contract management.

Contracts and the Dynamics of the Script

You will recall from Chapter 6 how the person may hold *compound script beliefs* in which one script belief is used to defend against another more damaging one. Examples:

'I can keep on living so long as I don't get close to anybody.'
'It's OK for me to exist, on condition that I work hard.'
'I can belong in a group, but only if I please other people.'

Reviewing the discussion in Chapter 6, you will see how a knowledge of compound decisions is important in contract-making. This knowledge will help you determine the order in which you invite the client to address different contract goals. In summary, the guidelines to follow are these:

* Do not invite *any* contract for script change until the client has closed escape hatches. There is always a possibility that any contract for a change in the script may uncover I Mustn't Exist. By closing escape hatches, the client takes protection against this risk.
* If you identify any possible compound beliefs, invite the client to move first to a contract to change the belief that is being defended against. Do not begin by addressing the belief that is being used as the defence. In the third of the examples above, you would begin by asking your client to take unconditional permission to feel at home in groups.

John: Contract-making and Treatment Direction

I have already described my assessment of the content of John's Racket System, including his possible compound beliefs (Chapter 6).

His presenting problem concerned mainly his difficulties in getting emotionally close to others. However, I had judged that he had been using his belief I Mustn't Be Close as a defence against I Mustn't Exist ('It's OK for me to stay alive as long as I don't get close to anybody').

John took a relatively long time to close escape hatches (Chapter 7). He did not close them until his eleventh session. I thus did not invite John to make any contract for script change until that time. However, during these earlier sessions we had agreed a series of contracts that were purely exploratory. John was able to bring his sharp thinking to bear in working out how he had been setting up painful outcomes for himself. He was able to use this knowledge to good advantage when he eventually did close the hatches and embarked upon script change.

By closing the escape hatches, John had taken Adult protection against I Mustn't Exist. Thus in planning how we might go on from that point, I judged that it would be safe for him to change the decision he had been using as a defence against I Mustn't Exist, namely I Mustn't Be Close. His first treatment contracts therefore centred on ways of getting appropriately close to others.

Self-supervision 8.1

CONTRACT-MAKING AND TREATMENT DIRECTION

Consider the client with whom you are working through the stages of the treatment sequence. In this self-supervision I am assuming that this client has closed escape hatches.

Consider the goals for change in counselling that you have discussed with your client. Bring these together with your knowledge of the details of her Racket System (Chapter 6). Use this combined evidence to make initial judgements about the following features of treatment direction. Questions to consider are:

1   Which are the principal script beliefs that the client will need to update in achieving the personal changes she has said she wants?
2   Do you have evidence that this may entail change in any compound beliefs? If so, which part of the compound belief will the client need to address first in contractual change? (Note: if the belief defended against is I Mustn't Exist, closure of the escape hatches will have given Adult protection under which the client can change the other part of the compound belief. However, I Mustn't Exist can always be addressed first in any case. It is usually therapeutic for the client to update this belief at some stage in treatment.)
3   Could she contract to express *feelings* different from the familiar ones she listed in the Racket System? Could she make a contract to update the archaic *thinking* represented by her script beliefs? How could she make a contractual change in one of the repetitive *behaviours* listed under rackety displays?

Overall Contract and Session Contract

Often, the client's stated contract goal will require some time for its achievement. His work to achieve it will thus extend over a number of counselling sessions. The contract for a major goal of this kind is usually called the *overall contract*.

To give increased direction to your work, it is usual to establish a shorter-term 'contract within a contract' which you and the client will address during any given session of counselling. This is known as a *session contract*. In the language of 'outcomes' and 'actions', described above, the overall contract will most often be for outcome, while session contracts are likely to be for actions which support that outcome.

The session contract must further the overall contract. For example, suppose the overall contract were 'I will take full permission to get close to people, in ways that are appropriate for me as a grown-up person. To mark this change, I will get on to first-name terms with four of the people I work with during the coming six months.' Possible session contracts might be:

'I will decide, by the end of this session, who is going to be the first person I get on first-name terms with.'

'I will put my mother in front of me in imagination and express to her how I feel about her childhood command to me not to be close to others.'

'I will go back in recollection to find whether I contact a scene from childhood when I was deciding I had to stay distant from others. If I do contact such a scene, I will change that old decision for an updated decision.'

The client may fulfil the session contract before the session ends. If so, it is important that you and he register the fact and go on to negotiate a further clear contract. For example, suppose the client has adopted the first of the possible session contracts listed above. Before the end of the session, he does clearly name a person he is going to approach. You might stroke the client for this change by saying 'Congratulations for being so clear about what you're going to do', then go on to ask 'Now what do you want to get from the rest of this session?'

Your client may say he wants to go on to another area of active change. Or perhaps he may prefer to take some quiet time in the remainder of the session to relax and simply 'be'. Either way, you and he stay clear about what is being agreed between you. By being explicit about your new contract, you have minimized the risk that you might move out of contractual work and into the pursuit of some hidden agenda.

Getting a clear session contract

Mary and Robert Goulding (1979) have stressed the importance of the opening moments of each session. This is the time when the real agenda for that session will be agreed upon between you and the client. You will either enter into a clear contract for change in the session, or will exchange psychological-level messages that reflect a covert agenda. If the latter takes place, the outcome is likely to be that the client furthers her script.

It is therefore important that you pay close attention to any ulterior messages that may be exchanged in the first few seconds of each session. You need to be alert to 'let-outs' of the kind outlined in the final section of this chapter.

You can also help achieve a clear session contract by opening with an explicit question about what the client wants from the session. Robert Goulding's classic opening question is:

'What do you want to change?'

Possible variants are:

'How do you want to change?'
'What do you want to have got for yourself by the end of this session?'

Openings like these help avoid the chance that you may slide into 'working on' problems or 'talking about' the client's issues. They create a mental set for active change. They help both you and your client to look forward to a desired outcome rather than backward to the problem.

Once your client gives you a clear statement of an objective to be achieved in the session, you may have to clarify with her how this session contract will serve to further her current overall contract.

Behavioural Assignments

You may suggest to the client that she carry out a particular behaviour between one session and the next. This is known as a *behavioural assignment*. The behaviour chosen will be one that furthers the current overall contract. For example, the client whose overall contract is 'to take permission to be close' might agree to a behavioural assignment: 'To address at least three workmates by their first names in the course of the week, and report back at the coming session.'

With behavioural assignments as with session contracts, it is necessary for you to invite the client's explicit Adult agreement to carry out any behaviours you suggest, and be attentive to make sure that her agreement is congruently given. Otherwise, you would not be working contractually.

Keeping Track of Contracts

To maintain a clear direction in treatment, it is necessary that you keep track of the progress of your client's contracts. I use the phrase *contract husbandry* to describe this careful tracking of contracts.

As you begin each session, you need to be aware of the overall contract you have in force with that client. Perhaps you and she agreed a session contract at the previous session. Was that contract achieved? If so, does she want to go on and do something in the present session that would further her movement out of script? If the past session's contract was not achieved, is the client going to continue addressing the same goal in today's session? Or will she abandon it and start a new one?

Did you agree a behavioural assignment at the last session? If you did, it is important that you ask the client how she has got on with it. If she has accomplished it, you can take the opportunity to stroke her. If not, you and she can examine how she stopped herself and discuss what she might do differently. If you do not ask her how she did, she may construe you in Child as either being uninterested in her or acquiescing to her staying in script.

As an aid to contract husbandry, you may keep written track of contracts. One useful way to do this is to make out a sheet of paper divided vertically into two columns. In the left-hand column you record the client's overall contract. In the right-hand column you list the relevant session contracts and behavioural assignments. You can date all these entries to show when each contract goal was first agreed and then either completed, renegotiated or abandoned.

Dealing With 'Sabotage'

Recall that in Child, your client will have been perceiving her script decisions as essential to getting needs met, even to her survival. Within this frame of reference, any movement out of script will appear to be a threat.

For this reason she is likely to find all sorts of ways of 'sabotaging' the contract-making process. I have placed the word 'sabotage' in quotation marks because for the client in Child, the motivation is exactly the opposite of sabotage. It is an attempt to cling to ways of getting by and surviving that served her well in early childhood. The 'sabotage' will be outside of her conscious awareness.

You therefore need to ensure that you and the client do not set off on a contract that covertly furthers the client's script. To achieve this you need to use your knowledge of life-script generally and the client's script in particular. As well as using Adult assessment, you need to use your intuition to tune in to the client's 'Martian' during the process of contract-making.

Some clients are most persistent in finding covert ways to slither out of a contract that threatens their script. In these circumstances you may feel tempted to go ahead and 'do counselling', even though you may not be clear what the contract goal is or whether it may further the client's script beliefs. On the occasions when I have done this, it has always turned out to be a mistake. Counsellor and client need to spend as much time as necessary to arrive at a clear, script-free contract. Without this, any work that follows will be built on shifting sands.

Here are some kinds of contract 'sabotage' that you are likely to meet, along with some suggestions on how to confront them.

Contract Furthering a Script Belief

Listen for clues that the content of the contract may further one of the beliefs in the client's script proper. For instance, a client may come to you saying 'I want help in keeping my feelings under control.'

Suppose that when you compile the details of his Racket System you find that 'I Mustn't Feel' is one of his script beliefs. You know from this that you would further his script if you accepted this contract.

Instead, you might invite the client to become aware that he has been repressing feelings. You and he might go on to agree a contract that helped him experience those feelings and express them safely and appropriately.

A similar caution applies to counterscript beliefs. An example might be the client who says 'I want help in getting more work done and making fewer mistakes.'

Suppose that, on investigating his counterscript, you find the beliefs 'I have to work hard' and 'I'm only acceptable if I get everything right'. To accept his proposed contract would simply be to assist him in digging himself deeper into his counterscript. The possible outcome for him might be that he suffered problems of stress or had a physical breakdown.

Instead, you can help your client be aware that his hard work and perfectionism are outdated strategies for getting needs met. You and he can work out another contract that allows him to meet those needs in a non-scripty way.

Contract Let-outs

There are numerous turns of phrase that betray ulterior 'sabotage' of a contract. To detect these, listen to the Martian – the literal content of what is being said – rather than what it is 'supposed' to mean in civilized company. Mary and Robert Goulding (1979) have emphasized how important it is to confront any of these 'let-outs' as soon as you hear it. If you ignore the let-out and go ahead on the basis of the social-level content, it is likely that your client in Child will use this to further her script. Here are some of the most frequent verbal let-outs:

- *'Work on'*   You ask the client 'What do you want to get by coming into counselling?'

  She replies: 'I want to work on my feelings of scare of authority figures.'

  This answer means just what it says. Though she is unaware of it, the client's covert intention is to use counselling sessions to interminably 'work on' a problem, rather than changing anything. You may counter this from Adult by bringing the Martian to the client's attention. A Child alternative (Goulding and Goulding, 1979) is to lean back in your chair, assume a posture of boredom and drone: 'Work on, and work on, and work on ...'
- *Hanging comparative*   Sometimes the client will say something like 'I've come for help in being more confident.' In this form of words, he uses the comparative 'more', but does not specify 'more than what'. Since the comparative is left 'hanging' in this way, neither you nor your client has any way of knowing how much more confident the client wants to become. The Child purpose of this let-out is similar to that of 'work on', namely to produce what the Gouldings call a 'forever contract'. To confront it, you can invite the client to give a sensory-based description of 'confident enough' behaviour.
- *'Try'*   This let-out usually appears towards the end of contract negotiation. You and the client seem to have agreed on a specific behavioural goal. You sum up by asking 'So will you ... (whatever the agreed action)?'

The client replies: 'Yes, I'll try.'

Again, the literal meaning is usually the real meaning. The client will *try* to do what he appears to be agreeing to. But he will not do it. If he did it, he wouldn't need to try to do it any more.

- *'Want to'*, *'Can'*, *'I think I will ...'*   All these have the same effect as 'try'. Most often, their literal meaning conveys what the client is actually saying. You can respond in the same way as to 'try': 'I hear that you'll try (you want to, you can, you think you will) do this. And will you?'

If the client then replies 'Yes, I will', watch out for incongruent non-verbal clues. They may communicate a psychological-level message from the client in Child: 'I'm saying the right thing now, but I've got my fingers crossed behind my back.'

All these let-outs indicate that your client in Child is defending against what she sees as a threat to her script beliefs.

In Chapter 9 I shall say more about how people defend their script beliefs. I shall suggest ways in which you can help your client to test these childhood beliefs against here-and-now reality. As he does so, he will move into active script change.

Further Reading in *Developing TA Counselling*

An entire section of *Developing TA Counselling* (Stewart, 1996a: Points 9 to 16) is devoted to further hints on effective contract-making.

9

CHALLENGING OUTDATED BELIEFS

Script Beliefs, Redefining and Discounting
Redefining Transactions
Discounting
The Discount Matrix
Confronting Rackets and Games
Further Reading in *Developing TA Counselling*

We saw in Chapters 3 and 6 that when a person is in script, she is replaying the self-limiting *script beliefs* she decided upon in childhood. Each time she does this, she is likely to repeat the maladaptive patterns of feeling and behaviour that make up her Racket System. An important focus for you in counselling, therefore, is to invite your client to test her script beliefs against here-and-now reality. To the extent that she does so and updates these old beliefs, she will move out of script and into autonomy.

Script Beliefs, Redefining and Discounting

Many of the interventions I describe in this chapter have been developed from an area of TA theory known as *Schiffian* or *Cathexis* theory. (For further detail of this theory, see Schiff et al., 1975; Stewart and Joines, 1987: 173–203.) In the 'Key Ideas' panel below, I outline some basic Schiffian concepts that relate to the practice described in this chapter.

Key Ideas 9.1

REDEFINING AND DISCOUNTING

1 When in script, the person distorts his perception of self, others and the world so that it fits his script beliefs. This process of distortion is called *redefining* (Mellor and Sigmund, 1975b). When the person is redefining, he is not consciously aware he is doing so.

2   The person redefines *intrapsychically* (that is, 'inside his own head'). Thus to judge whether he may be redefining, you need to go on the evidence of certain clues that the person shows externally. Among these clues are certain patterns of communication called *redefining transactions*. I give examples in a later section.

3   As part of the process of redefining, the person may engage in *discounting* (Mellor and Sigmund, 1975a). This is defined as *ignoring or minimizing certain features of reality*. In discounting, the person typically underestimates his own or other people's resources, or ignores some of the options available in the real-life situation. He does this without conscious awareness.

4   Like redefining, discounting is carried on intrapsychically. Thus to judge whether someone may be discounting, you need to depend on the evidence of clues that the person may show externally. These clues may be verbal or non-verbal. They may be found in the person's behaviour, in his expression of feeling, or in his reported thinking. I give examples of such clues throughout the chapter.

In the first two main sections of this chapter, I describe in turn how you can detect and confront redefining transactions and the verbal and non-verbal clues to discounting. In the next section we look at the *Discount Matrix*. This is a model that you can use to pinpoint the nature and intensity of discounting.

The final section shows how you can confront script beliefs by confronting the rackety displays that accompany them (recall the Racket System, Chapter 3).

You will see that the layout of this chapter is symmetrical with that of Chapter 6. In the earlier chapter, we looked at how you could gather information on your client's script beliefs and rackety displays. Now in this chapter, we consider how you can confront those script beliefs and rackety displays.

Chapters 9 and 10 and the treatment sequence

Chapters 9 and 10 both describe ways in which you can help your client to update script beliefs, resolve script feelings, and move out of scripty behaviours. The difference in focus between the two chapters relates to the principal *ego-state* in which your client will be during the process of change. The present chapter describes techniques in which your client will be mainly in the Adult ego-state. In Chapter 10 we shall look at interventions by which you invite the client to make changes while he is in Child.

The order of these two chapters reflects the treatment sequence recommended by Eric Berne (1961). In current practice, the transactional analyst will move flexibly back and forth between these two classes of intervention according to the treatment contract and the needs of the client (cf. Mellor, 1980b).

The Nature and Functions of Confrontation

Throughout the chapter I shall be speaking of *confronting* script beliefs. I think it is worth repeating here that in TA usage, the word 'confrontation' does not imply harsh or aggressive intervention. To 'confront' is simply to speak or act in any way that invites your client to place her script beliefs face to face with reality.

Indeed, if you are to be fully effective in your confrontations, you have to deliver them from a position of 'I'm OK, you're OK'. You are confronting the person's scripty patterns of belief, feeling and action, not questioning the worth of the person herself.

Confrontation and updating

When you confront one of your client's script beliefs she has only three courses open to her:

* To reject or ignore your confrontation and continue to replay the same script belief.
* To evade your confrontation by switching to another of her script beliefs. In that event, you can shift with her and begin confronting the alternative belief.
* To accept your confrontation without switching to an alternative belief. This necessarily means she will replace the script belief with a perception of here-and-now reality.

You may help this process along by giving the person reality-based information.

Redefining Transactions

In TA terminology, a *transaction* simply means any exchange of communications between two people (Berne, 1966: 370). In a *redefining transaction*, the person who responds 'shifts the ground' of what is being discussed. He does this without awareness. His motive always is that, in Child, he perceives the original topic as a threat to his script beliefs. To defend against this, he redefines internally. He then responds out of the redefinition.

In counselling, confronting the client's script beliefs is one of your main purposes. Thus people are especially prone to engage in redefining transactions during a counselling session. The covert purpose of this is to divert the attention of both of you from the original issue that threatened the person's script beliefs.

By shifting ground in this way, your client is issuing a Child invitation to you to accompany him on to his new tack. If you accept his invitation, your client is likely to experience you as having 'confirmed' his redefinition and hence his script beliefs.

There are two types of redefining transaction. They are the *tangential transaction* and the *blocking transaction*.

Tangential Transactions

Let us call the two parties to a transaction Person A and Person B. In a *tangential transaction*, person B 'shifts the ground' by *addressing a different issue from the one that Person A originally raised*, or addressing the same issue from a different perspective. Example:

COUNSELLOR: What do you want to get from our sessions together?
CLIENT: Well, people often tell me I should be more assertive.

Here the ground has been shifted from 'what the client wants' to 'what people tell him'. The Child invitation is for you to open a discussion about how he might become more assertive. This would divert attention from your original request to him, which was to say what *he* wants.

Sometimes you will detect a tangential transaction by paying attention to the person's choice of words:

COUNSELLOR: How do you feel?
CLIENT: I feel maybe you're laughing at me.

The client uses the word 'feel', but what follows is a report of a perception, not a feeling. This client may be replaying the script belief that revealing feelings is dangerous. Were you to go with his invitation and tell him whether or not you were laughing at him, you would leave that belief unconfronted.

Sometimes the tangential move may be simply to leave a question unanswered:

CLIENT: ... so when she said that to me, I felt really irritated.
COUNSELLOR: How are you feeling now?
CLIENT: Trouble was, I couldn't bring myself to tell her ...

During a session you may sometimes have felt a vague sensation of the ground having shifted under your feet. If so, one possibility is that you missed a redefining response and went off on a tangent with your client. Some people in Child are highly skilled at issuing tangential responses, even though the skill is outside of their awareness. If you do not confront, you may spend most of the session following the client from one new tack to the next. At the end of a session like this you may feel drained, as though you have been using a lot of energy but somehow have been going round in circles, getting nowhere.

Blocking Transactions

A *blocking transaction* is one in which *the purpose of raising an issue is avoided by disagreeing about the definition of the issue.* Examples:

COUNSELLOR: What do you want to get from our sessions together?
CLIENT: Ah, well! I'm wondering if it's really a matter of what I want to get.

Or:

COUNSELLOR: How do you feel?
CLIENT: Do you mean how do I feel emotionally, or what feelings I have in my body?

In a blocking transaction, the Child tactic is to engage you in an argument over definitions. This would divert attention from the perceived threat to the person's script beliefs.

Confronting Redefining Transactions

For effective intervention, you have to be aware of *every* redefining response by your client. You may choose to confront immediately. Alternatively, you may wait for a few more transactions to see whether the content of the redefinition gives you insight into the client's script beliefs. If you take the latter course, it is important to hold clearly in your mind what topic you were on before the redefinition. In either event, at some point you need to get back on the original tack and invite your client to join you. One standard way is simply to repeat your question verbatim:

COUNSELLOR: What do you want to get from our sessions together?
CLIENT: Well, people often tell me I should be more assertive.
COUNSELLOR: What do you want to get from our sessions together?

You may repeat your question several times if the client continues to redefine.

Another approach is to make a meta-comment about the redefinition:

COUNSELLOR: How do you feel?
CLIENT: I feel maybe you're laughing at me.
COUNSELLOR: Seems to me you were saying to yourself 'This guy is laughing at me.' That's a belief, not a feeling. So, how are you *feeling*?

Or:

COUNSELLOR: How are you feeling now?
CLIENT: Trouble was, I couldn't bring myself to tell her . . .
COUNSELLOR: You didn't answer my question. Will you answer me?

In response to a blocking move, you can often confront successfully by handing the responsibility for definitions back to the client:

COUNSELLOR: How do you feel?
CLIENT: Do you mean how do I feel emotionally, or what feelings I have in my body?
COUNSELLOR: Whichever!

You have already met examples like these in Chapters 7 and 8, though I did not use the word 'redefining' at those points. For instance, from the discussion of contract-making in Chapter 8:

COUNSELLOR: So will you do what we've just agreed?
CLIENT: Yes, I'll try to.

You will see now that this 'let-out' is an example of a redefining transaction. By his reply, the client shifts the topic away from what he *will* do.

Instead, he speaks about what he will *try* to do. In addressing this let-out, the counsellor confronts the redefinition:

COUNSELLOR: Well, I wasn't asking you what you were going to 'try' to do. I was asking you what you are going to do.

Again, during the procedure for closing escape hatches (Chapter 7), you might typically hear an exchange like this:

COUNSELLOR: Will you undertake never to kill or harm yourself under any circumstances?
CLIENT: Oh, I'm too much of a coward! I don't have the courage to hurt myself.
COUNSELLOR: [*Confronts*] So are you saying that one of these days, if you just get up enough courage, you may hurt yourself?

Thus during contract-making, and earlier when the client was closing escape hatches, you have already been confronting redefining transactions.

Self-supervision 9.1

REDEFINING TRANSACTIONS

From a recent session with your chosen client, pick out a segment of tape a few minutes in length. Listen to it several times through and note the following:

1 At what points did your client offer you a redefining response? For each of these points note:

   – as it a tangential or a blocking transaction?
   – Did you go with the client into the redefinition, or confront?
   – If you confronted, did you do so immediately or wait?
   – If you went with the redefinition, what did you and your client do next?

2 Which of your interventions on this tape do you think were particularly effective?
3 Finally, summarize what you will do differently next time.

Discounting

In the opening section of this chapter I explained that when the person discounts, she does so intrapsychically. Thus discounting itself is not directly observable. Instead, you have to infer when the person is discounting, using the evidence of external clues that you can observe. These clues may lie in the person's choice of words or in her non-verbal signals.

Each time other people appear to 'confirm' the internal discount, the person is likely to use this outside of awareness to justify her script beliefs. Thus it is important that you confront your client's discounts. This means *consistently* drawing to her attention the way she minimizes features of herself, others or the situation. She may battle against your confrontations, because they threaten the old beliefs which in Child she perceives as necessary for her survival. In many subtle ways, and without conscious intention, she is likely to invite you to stroke her discounts. You need to look out for these invitations and decline each one.

With discounts, as with redefining transactions, it is not always necessary that you confront immediately. You may choose on occasions to make a mental note of the discount and wait to see what follows. But for potent work, you do need to be *aware* of each and every discount.

There are innumerable ways in which people show they may be discounting, and many ways also in which different transactional analysts go about confronting discounts. In the space available here, I cannot list all of these. I will simply give examples from which I hope you can develop a general 'feel' for the process of confrontation. You can use this to work out your own preferred techniques through experience.

Verbal Clues to Discounting

Here are a few examples of how the person's choice of words can indicate she is probably discounting:

'I can't think.'
'You're making me feel bad.'
'It's uncomfortable to do that.' *(Meaning 'I'm uncomfortable'.)*
'I'm no good without you.'
'I see you can't spell.'
'Can you tell me how you're feeling?' *(Assuming the person addressed has no physical or speech disability, it's obvious she 'can' say how she is feeling. The question is, will she?)*
'People can't be trusted these days.'

'We had no alternative but to go on strike.'
'Life is just one big struggle.'

Thinking back to the verbal 'let-outs' you met in Chapters 7 and 8 you will recognize now that many of these also were clues to discounting.

Distortion and deletion

Verbal clues to discounting include *deletion* as well as *distortion* (cf. Bandler and Grinder, 1975). In deletion, the person misses out information that would be relevant to solving a problem. Examples:

'I want to get close *(Deletion: close to whom?)*, but I can't *(distortion)*.'
'I need help.' *(Deletions: help with what? from whom?)*
'People *(Deletion: which people?)* are out to get me *(distortion)*.'
'I want you to tell me how you feel.' *(Deletion: the speaker has implied a request to the other person to tell him how she feels, but has not made the request explicit. To fill in the deletion, the speaker would need to add a phrase like 'So will you?', or simply ask 'Will you tell me how you feel?')*

Detecting verbal clues to discounting

In principle, it is simple to detect verbal clues to discounting. You have evidence of discounting *whenever the person says anything that indicates she is ignoring or diminishing some aspect of reality.* The 'aspect of reality' in question may relate to herself, to others, or to the here-and-now situation.

In practice there are two difficulties. The first is that everyday social conversation is loaded with verbal discounts, so much so that most of us become desensitized to them. You can remedy this by building up your skill in 'thinking Martian' (recall Chapter 1). Your aim is to step outside the conventions of what people's words are supposed to mean, and hear instead what they are actually saying.

The second difficulty is that when people discount, they do so outside of their awareness. Every discount represents a 'blind spot' for the person, that is, a feature of reality that he is ignoring without conscious intention. *If you do not share the same blind spot*, you will have no difficulty in picking up the discount. But if you do share that blind spot, then by definition you will also miss the discount, and you will not be consciously aware you are missing it.

This underlines how important it is for you to resolve your own script issues in counselling or therapy. By doing so you reduce the number of your own blind spots. You can supplement this by regular supervision on your counselling work, picking out with hindsight when your client was discounting and whether you confronted.

Evaluating the Discount

One way to confront verbal discounts is by inviting your client to bring his Adult functioning to bear in evaluating the nature of the discount. Examples:

CLIENT: You see, I'm just a naturally stand-offish person.
COUNSELLOR: Do you think it's really true that you're 'naturally' that way?

CLIENT: I need help.
COUNSELLOR: Help with what?

When you hear the initial discount, you may probe to discover in more detail what script beliefs the client is replaying. By doing this you may be able to reach the earliest and most catastrophic belief against which the client has been defending in Child. You can then direct your confrontation at that belief. In this example, the counsellor uses sentence completion as a means of probing:

CLIENT: I just couldn't tell my mother how angry I feel at her.
COUNSELLOR: 'Because if I did tell her, I'm scared that … '?
CLIENT: I'm scared she wouldn't be able to cope with it.
COUNSELLOR: 'And if I'm angry with her and she can't cope with it, I'm scared in case … '?
CLIENT: [Pause] I'm scared in case she just falls to pieces.
COUNSELLOR: You're scared that if you're angry with your mother, she'll fall to pieces?
CLIENT: Yes.
COUNSELLOR: Sounds to me like you may have been believing 'If I show my mother I'm angry with her, I'll destroy her.' Do you think you have been believing that?
CLIENT: Yes, I think I probably have.
COUNSELLOR: So what's the reality? (This is a useful question to ask when you hear a script belief.)

CLIENT: I can be angry with her, and she'll survive.
COUNSELLOR: Say that again?
CLIENT: I can be angry with her, and she'll survive.
COUNSELLOR: Yeah, you're right, she'll survive. *(Confirms the reality-based perception.)* I think you just did a good bit of updating for yourself.

Contradicting the Discount

A different way of confronting is simply to give out a direct contradiction of the discount. Examples:

CLIENT: I can't think.
COUNSELLOR: Yes, you can!

CLIENT: You're making me feel angry!
COUNSELLOR: No, I'm not. It's not possible for anybody to 'make you' feel anything.

If you are not accustomed to using direct contradiction, it may seem at first sight to be an intrusion on the client. However, the rationale for it becomes clearer from the following story (told by Shea Schiff, workshop presentation). A little boy rushes into Daddy's bedroom: 'Daddy! Daddy! There's a tiger under my bed!'

Now it might seem that the caring thing for Daddy to do would be to take the little boy back into his bedroom and look under the bed. He might ask the boy to look there with him to check that there really was no tiger.

But if Daddy did that, he would be 'confirming' his son's belief that there *might* sometimes be tigers under little boys' beds. Because, if not, why bother to look for them there?

So a better way for Daddy to respond would be to say firmly: 'There are *no* tigers under little boys' beds. You're safe. Now, go back to bed.'

This story highlights the ego-states that counsellor and client are employing during this kind of confrontation. The counsellor issues his contradiction as a *definition of reality*, using the words and non-verbal signals that indicate a Parent ego-state. He invites the client to hear his definition in Child. This is in contrast to what happens when you ask a client to evaluate a discount (section above); in that case, you and the client engage Adult to Adult.

It need hardly be said that you should reserve such direct contradiction for use when your client says something that clearly *does* ignore or diminish some aspect of reality. You would typically use it in response to a discount like 'I can't think'. In cases like these, the client is stating a self-limiting script belief *as though it were a fact*. The reality is that the client *can* think. Maybe he has not been fully using his ability to think, or maybe he believes he can't think, but these are different matters. Therefore it is legitimate for you, like Daddy in the story, to take up a Parental stance and simply tell your client how things are.

Confronting Incongruity

The selection of 'non-verbal let-outs' given in the chapters on closing escape hatches and on contract-making (Chapters 7 and 8) are all examples of non-verbal clues to discounting. You know that you detect such clues by watching out for *incongruity*: body signals not matching the content of what the person is saying.

In practice, you can never be certain whether a particular non-verbal signal does indicate that the person is discounting. Recall from Chapter 7 the person who puts his hand in front of his mouth while saying he will never kill or harm others. Intuitively, you may guess that his gesture denies his words, and thus signals a discount. But since you cannot read his mind, you need to check your initial judgement by questioning.

If you are in doubt about the meaning of non-verbal signals, *always* check verbally whether the person is discounting. *Never* just go ahead on the evidence of the social-level content. The rationale for this lies in Berne's 'rule of communication' (Chapter 1): it is the psychological level of communication that tells us what is really going on. Thus if the person *is* discounting and you assume he is not, you will misjudge the entire meaning of whatever passes between you.

Until you know whether your client is inviting you to stroke her script, your best option may temporarily be to do and say *nothing*. Anything you do or say may be taken down mentally by your client and used as 'evidence' for her script beliefs. This may apply even to seemingly neutral responses on your part such as 'Mhm', a smile or a change in facial expression.

Confronting gallows

A frequent clue to discounting is the incongruity called *gallows*. In this the person laughs or smiles while talking about something painful. Examples:

'Oh, ha ha, what an idiot I am!'
'I really don't think I *can* cut down on my drinking.' *(Smiles.)*

The gallows is a Child invitation to you to join in the laugh or return the smile. If you do, the other person is likely to construe you as having confirmed her discount.

To confront gallows, you refrain from joining in with your client's laughter. Instead of smiling, you remain stony-faced. You can also repudiate the discount in words:

CLIENT: I had a bit of a bang in the car on my way down here today, ha ha!
COUNSELLOR: [*Unsmiling*] That's not funny.

Not all laughter is gallows. Further, a gallows laugh does not necessarily *sound* any different from a straight laugh. How do you tell the difference? The answer is that you need to judge from context. If in doubt, be cautious about joining in with laughing or smiling until you find out what your client is doing internally.

Self-supervision 9.2

CONFRONTING DISCOUNTS

Take a segment of tape a few minutes long from a recent session with your client. Listen to it several times through. Consider the following questions:

1 At what points do you now hear clues that your client may have been discounting? For each instance that you hear, go on to note:

   – How was the discount signalled: verbally or by non-verbal clues such as gallows laughing?
   – Did you confront?
   – If you confronted, did your client register acceptance of your confrontation?
   – Any other options you could have used in confronting?
   – If you did not confront, what did your client do next?

2 Note the features of your work that you judge were particularly effective.

3 Finally, summarize anything you will do differently next time.

The Discount Matrix

The *Discount Matrix* is a model that allows you to pinpoint the nature and intensity of a person's discounting (Mellor and Sigmund, 1975a). It is designed to assist in both the formulation and the solution of problems. The model begins by distinguishing three *areas* of discounting:

- self
- others
- the situation.

In one statement he made to me, John expressed discounts in all three areas:

'I just can't tell my parents how I feel about them.' *(Discount of self.)*
'But then, they're not the kind of people you can talk to.' *(Discount of the other.)*
'And anyway, in our family it's just not on for people to say how they feel.' *(Discount of the situation.)*

Within each area, discounts are next classified into four *levels* and three *types* (Mellor and Sigmund used the term 'mode' instead of 'level'). This gives a four-by-three matrix. It is shown in Figure 9.1.

Each box on the matrix represents a particular combination of type and level of discount. Taking the top left-hand box as an example: level is *existence*; type is *stimuli*. When a person discounts the existence of stimuli, he is blanking out his sensory awareness of something that is going on, either internally or externally. Example: the person who neither feels hungry before eating nor feels full afterwards.

In the next box to the right, the person is discounting the *existence of problems*. Here she is aware something is going on, but is blanking out the possibility that it may be a problem for her or for someone. Example: the mother who hears baby crying and says: 'Ah, there's the baby crying again. Babies always cry.'

Moving one place further right, the person discounting the *existence of options* will realize that something is going on and that it may be a problem, but will ignore the possibility that there is any action available to solve the problem. Example: someone is driving a car fast down the motorway in fog. Without slackening speed, he says to his passenger: 'Nasty fog, eh? I see they've got the speed-limit signs on.'

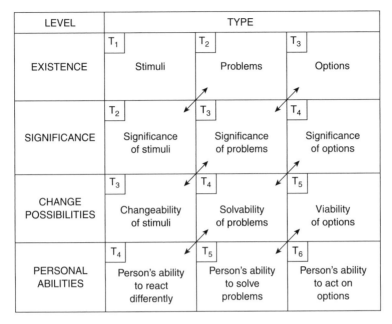

LEVEL	TYPE		
EXISTENCE	T₁ Stimuli	T₂ Problems	T₃ Options
SIGNIFICANCE	T₂ Significance of stimuli	T₃ Significance of problems	T₄ Significance of options
CHANGE POSSIBILITIES	T₃ Changeability of stimuli	T₄ Solvability of problems	T₅ Viability of options
PERSONAL ABILITIES	T₄ Person's ability to react differently	T₅ Person's ability to solve problems	T₆ Person's ability to act on options

Figure 9.1   The Discount Matrix

Moving one row down on the matrix: when someone discounts the *significance of stimuli*, she is aware that something is going on, but blocks out any realization that it may have some meaning for her. Once again as an example here, we can cite the mother who hears baby crying and says 'Babies always cry.'

The rest of the matrix is constructed by continuing this process. You may like to take one of the examples above and work out how you might detect the person discounting at the various other combinations of type and level.

The Hierarchy of Discounts

There are inter-relationships between the boxes in the Discount Matrix. A discount in any box *also entails discounts in*:

- all the boxes to its *right*
- all the boxes *below* it
- all the boxes *on the same diagonal.*

This principle is called the *hierarchy of discounts.*

Example: if a person is not aware of feeling hungry or feeling full, she will also not perceive she has any problem to solve in acting to assuage these feelings (box to the right). Since she does not perceive a problem, she has no motive to consider options to solve that problem (two boxes right).

By blanking out her awareness of the sensations of hunger and fullness, this person also blanks out any question of the sensations having some meaning for her (one box below). Again you may care to complete the example for the other boxes in the matrix.

We have already noted that the mother with the crying baby, who was discounting the existence of a problem, was by the same token discounting the significance of the stimulus. These two boxes are on the same diagonal. Notice that on the matrix diagram the diagonals are shown by arrows and are given numbers from T1 (top left) to T6 (bottom right). From the hierarchy of discounts you will realize that:

- a discount on any diagonal also entails discounts *on all diagonals below it and to its right.*

Once again you may want to confirm this using one of the examples above.

Using the Discount Matrix in Problem Formulation

When anyone is failing to solve a problem, this is because he is missing some of the information that could lead him to effective action. The usefulness of the Discount Matrix in problem formulation is that it helps you pinpoint the position of this 'missing link' in the person's information.

The Discount Matrix was designed primarily for use where the person has access to the necessary information but is blanking it out of awareness (discounting). However, it can be used just as effectively for problems that arise through *lack of information* or *misinformation.* Thus the Discount Matrix is an effective tool for use in a wide range of counselling settings where script issues may not be addressed, for example, in career counselling.

When a person says or does something that indicates she is discounting, your first action is to locate the type and mode of the discount on the matrix. However, this first impression may not tell you accurately where the underlying 'missing link' in her information lies. Why? Because *she may also be discounting on a diagonal above and to the left of the discount you first notice.*

John: Hierarchy of Discounts

One of John's stated wants was to get emotionally closer to his parents. I accepted this as a generalized contract goal, since I saw it as marking a movement out of his early decision not to be close. As we negotiated what specific change this contract might mean for John, I used the Discount Matrix to pinpoint how he had been discounting (session thirteen).

John began by stating his problem: 'I can't seem to talk to my parents about any kind of feelings.' At first sight, he appeared to be discounting his own ability to act on options. This would have placed his discount on diagonal T6. However, I checked this first impression by questioning, working systematically up the diagonals on the matrix. Here is how the exchange went on:

JOHN: I want to get closer to my parents, but there seems to be no way I can do it.

COUNSELLOR: What's one action you could take in the coming week, so that at the end of the week you could say, 'Yes, I *have* got closer to my parents in the way I want?' *(Investigates T5)*

JOHN: [*Pause*] Actually, I don't know if there's anything in particular I could do about that. *(Indicates discount on T5)*

COUNSELLOR: So, at the moment you're not thinking of anything in particular you can do. Do you reckon you have it in you to actually get closer to your parents in the way you want? *(Investigates T4)*

JOHN: [*Gallows smile*] Well, maybe when it comes down to it, I don't know if I have. Maybe I'm just not the sort of person who can get close to other people. *(Discounting on T4)*

COUNSELLOR: Do you know anybody else who's ever got close to their parents in the way you want to do? *(Investigates T3)*

JOHN: Oh, sure! Helen does, for a start.

John's 'missing link' was revealed as lying not at T6 but at T4. In the area of self, he had been discounting his own ability to react differently. This meant he had also been discounting the solvability of his problem and the significance of any options he had available.

At the same time, he and I had discovered that our frames of reference matched at T3. We were now able to use this common ground as our joint starting point in working out a solution to the problem.

In problem formulation you can equally well take the other route into the Discount Matrix, beginning at the top left and working downwards on the diagonals. You may like to compose your own example of this.

Interventions on the Discount Matrix

As well as helping in the formulation of problems, the Discount Matrix is a guide to effective intervention. The principle to follow is this:

* discover on what diagonal the client is discounting, and intervene *on or above that diagonal* in the Discount Matrix.

If you make your intervention on a lower diagonal than this, the intervention itself is likely to be discounted.

John: Interventions on the Discount Matrix

To continue the example in the previous section: suppose I had gone with my initial impression, and directed my intervention at T6, 'ability to act on options'. I might have invited John to go ahead and open some approaches to his parents in the coming week, and come back and report to me. On the social level, he might have agreed to do this. However, he had in fact been discounting at T4, not T6. Internally, he had been blanking out any recognition of specific actions he could take that would count as 'getting closer to his parents' (T5). What was more, he had been minimizing his own inherent ability to do *anything* to achieve the outcome he said he wanted (T4). Thus, so long as I continued to intervene at T6, the chances were that John would have found ways of continuing to sabotage his agreed change.

I therefore confronted first at the highest diagonal on which John had been discounting, T4. I planned that if I was successful in this move, I would then shift to T5 and in the same way to T6. Finally, I would invite John out of the matrix at the bottom right-hand corner. With this, he would move into active problem-solving.

This is how our exchange went on:

COUNSELLOR: OK, so you know there's at least one other person who can do what you want to do. Well, here's some information for you. You *are* 'the sort of person who can get close to other people'. You have that ability, just like Helen has and like lots of other people have. *(Direct contradiction of the discount on T4)*

JOHN: When you put it straight out like that, yes, of course I can see I have the ability. But I still *feel* I can't get close to people.

COUNSELLOR: That's different. 'Feeling you can't' is different from 'not being able to'. *(Repeats contradiction on T4)*

JOHN: [*Laughs*] Yeah, you have a point there! *(Moves out of discount on T4)* [*Pause*] But the trouble is still, I just can't think how I could make any kind of opening to talk to my parents about how I feel. Can you give me any ideas what to do about that? *(Discounting on T5)*

COUNSELLOR: I'm going to turn that question back to you. What's one thing you could do in the coming week that would be 'making an opening to talk to your parents?' *(Asks client to evaluate discount on T5)*

By the end of this session, John had moved to T6 and then out of the Discount Matrix into a contract for problem-solving. He had registered that it was open to him to telephone his parents and fix a time when he could go and visit them, rather than wait for them to contact him, as he had usually done in the past. He also recognized that since his parents were not given to opening discussions about feelings, he would need to broach this subject himself. His final step was to contract with me that he would actually take these actions in the week that followed, and report back to me at our next session.

In the event, John carried out this contract. For the first time as an adult, he shared with his parents how he felt about them. After some initial discomfort, their response was to open up in return. By this active step in problem-solving, John was able to register in

Adult that neither he nor his parents were as he had pictured them in his script beliefs. Each time he repeated the new behaviour, he would weaken one of the main feedback loops in his Racket System. In its place he would strengthen a new loop, this time appropriate to the reality of his options as an adult.

Treatment Planning and the Discount Matrix

The examples above have illustrated how you can use the Discount Matrix as a guide both to treatment sequence (Chapter 2) and to contract-making (Chapter 8). Beginning with the problem as the client presents it, you first discover the highest diagonal on which she is discounting. You then work out contracts that will address the diagonals in order, starting at that highest diagonal and working downwards. In particular, this helps avoid the temptation to jump prematurely to a behavioural contract that might miss a discount higher in the matrix. Example: for the client who did not register feelings of hunger or fullness, your first contract might be for her to spend some weeks simply paying attention to the sensations in her body before and after eating, noting these sensations and talking about them to you.

Self-supervision 9.3

USING THE DISCOUNT MATRIX

It may be instructive to use the same tape segment as you used for self-supervision 9.2 (confronting discounts). Listening several times through, note for each clue to discounting that you hear:

1 In what area is the discount (self, others, the situation)?
2 Within that area, which box in the Discount Matrix does the discount fit in (what is its type and level)?
3 If you confront, which diagonal in the matrix do you address with your confrontation?
4 How does this compare to the diagonal on which your client is discounting?
5 What does your client do next?
6 What do you judge was effective about what you did this time?
7 Anything you will do differently next time?

Confronting Rackets and Games

You will recall that you met *rackets* and *games* in Chapter 6. All rackets and games are external manifestations that the person is replaying her script beliefs intrapsychically. That is, she is discounting. To help your client move out of script, your task is to confront these old patterns and present new options in their place.

Your client's initial complaint will probably concern rackets and games she is playing with people outside the counselling relationship. However, she is likely to parallel this by playing out the same patterns within your sessions. You can direct your interventions at either focus.

Working With Racket Feelings

In counselling, your aim is to convey to your client that she no longer needs to follow the magical strategies she decided on in infancy. As a grown-up, she has better ways of arranging to get her needs met. You can communicate this by:

* confronting rackety behaviours and racket feelings
* stroking problem-solving behaviours and authentic feelings
* making sure you do *not* stroke rackets or racket feelings.

One point immediately follows. It is that *the ventilation of feelings, in itself, is not necessarily therapeutic.* If your client ventilates racket feelings and you stroke him for this, he will construe you as having confirmed his script beliefs. Bob Goulding (workshop presentation) has pointed out the fallacy of believing that everybody has a 'barrel of feelings', and that to get better they only need to keep on ventilating until the barrel is emptied. The truth is, says Goulding, that the barrel may turn out to be bottomless. If the feelings being expressed are racket feelings, the person can keep on expressing them *ad infinitum* and nothing will change.

Avoiding touch-stroking racket feelings

The Gouldings emphasize in particular that it is important to *avoid touching a client* when she is ventilating a racket feeling (Goulding and Goulding, 1979: 97). When, for example, someone bursts into tears during a session and reaches out for physical contact, it may seem 'natural' and 'caring' to take her hand or hold her. But touching is a potent stroke for the Child. Thus if this client's tears are expressing racket sadness and you touch her in response, she is most likely to take this as 'confirmation' of a script belief.

Your action instead could be to invite her into the authentic feeling she has been covering with the racket.

'Peeling the onion'

But how do you facilitate your client into shifting from the racket feeling into an authentic feeling? Often the way to do this is to give her time *initially* to 'blow off steam' in expression of the racket feeling. After a while she may often move spontaneously into the authentic feeling. You can help this process if you keep careful watch for body signals.

Example: a client is shouting out his rage against his father, placed in fantasy on an empty cushion. You know he has done this several times before and experienced no lasting relief, so your hypothesis is that his anger is a racket feeling.

CLIENT: [*Yells*] I'm angry at you, Dad! [*Beats cushion*]
COUNSELLOR: Again. (*Invites continued expression without stroking the feeling being expressed*)
CLIENT: [*Voice becomes low; hides face in hands*] I'm angry at you, Dad.
COUNSELLOR: You don't sound angry. [*Confronts incongruity*] Give yourself time now to feel whatever you feel. [*Strokes shift to authentic feeling*] [*Pause*] Now go ahead and tell Dad what you're feeling.
CLIENT: I'm scared. I'm scared of being angry at you, Dad.

The client has shifted into authentic scare, which he had been covering with racket anger. If he is ready, you and he can now begin to explore what it is he has been scared of, and discover what he needs to do to resolve his fears.

Sometimes the person will cover one racket feeling with another, or with several others. Thus in counselling you may need to start with the racket feeling the client first presents, and work inwards in the manner of 'peeling an onion'. Often the layers of racket feelings will come from different developmental stages, with the feelings learned at later stages on the 'outside of the onion'. The client in our example first presented with a racket of blankness. Under stress his initial reaction was to stop himself experiencing any emotion at all. With time and confrontation by the counsellor, he became willing to let himself feel his underlying anger. Finally he reached his authentic Child feeling of scare.

To sum up: it is never therapeutic to stroke a racket feeling. But it may be therapeutic to invite your client to ventilate a racket feeling for a time, when you believe this will provide her with a way through to the underlying authentic feeling. Your task is to stay aware of when your client is in a racket feeling and when she is showing an authentic feeling, and to be choosy about which of these you stroke.

This shift from racket to authentic feeling is a central feature of the change process known as *redecision* (see Chapter 10).

Confronting the Myth of Make-feel

If someone is experiencing a racket feeling, she can always move out of it simply by choosing to feel another feeling instead.

A personal example: for most of my life, one of my single-handed rackets has been to 'lose' my car key, usually when I have been in a hurry to go somewhere. Outside of my awareness, my purpose in setting this up was to justify myself in feeling racket irritation. Since learning about rackets, I have used a different strategy. Now if I 'misplace' my key, I tell myself: 'Aha! I notice I've just got into this racket set-up again.' In place of racket irritation, I choose to feel pleased with myself for having been clever enough to spot the racket.

Interestingly, a by-product of this has been that I now 'lose' my keys less often than I used to. And when viewed in terms of the Racket System, this is the result that would be expected. By choosing to stroke myself for cleverness and feel pleased, instead of criticizing myself and feeling irritated, I have interrupted the old rackety loop called for in my script. Thus the feeling change in itself helps extinguish the rackety behaviour.

What happens when you offer your clients this strategy? In my experience, many people have difficulty at first in believing that they can choose how they feel. Most of us are taught in childhood that it is other people, or external events, that *cause* us to feel what we feel. The Gouldings call this the *myth of make-feel* (Goulding and Goulding, 1979). This myth is perpetuated by many cultural influences, including popular songs ('You made me love you … ').

When a person believes that external events make her feel, then she is also believing that she has no power to decide how she feels. Perhaps this is one reason why people in adulthood may cling tenaciously to the myth of make-feel. It is a magical Child means of handing responsibility for feelings over to the environment. By discounting her own power in this way, the person is also able to believe that her scripty responses are 'caused' by the environment, rather than being her own choice.

In counselling, your task is consistently to confront the myth of make-feel each time the client expresses it. I have given several examples in the section above on 'Confronting Discounts'. Here are a couple more:

> CLIENT: This whole situation is so frustrating!
> COUNSELLOR: You're feeling frustrated in this situation. Do you hear the difference between the way I said it and the way you said it? *(Confronts make-feel; invites client to evaluate the discount)*
>
> CLIENT: Now you're getting me confused.
> COUNSELLOR: Test saying: 'Ian, I'm bloody angry at you!' *(A double confrontation. I deny make-feel, and invite the client to express the authentic feeling which I guess he may have been covering by racket confusion)*

Confronting Racketeering

From Chapter 6 you will recall the process called *racketeering* (English, 1976a, 1976b). This happens when one person invites another to stroke him for exhibiting racket feelings. The invitation will be issued on the psychological level. Here is an imaginary example:

> CLIENT: I had another row with my boss today, and I'm feeling really down in the mouth about it.
> COUNSELLOR: *[In error]* Dear, dear. I'm so sorry to hear you're feeling that way.
> CLIENT: Yes, and the trouble is, I don't know what I can say to him that will make any difference.
> COUNSELLOR: *[In error]* When you say that, I really feel for you.

On the psychological level, the client's invitation is: 'Please stroke me for feeling depressed and helpless.' The counsellor in the example buys into the invitation with his responses, and the racketeering is under way.

People can racketeer either from Parent or from Child ego-states. English subdivides Child racketeers into two classes that she calls 'Helpless' and 'Bratty'. The Helpless racketeer sounds sad and doleful, like the client in our example. Bratty, like Helpless, is played from a one-down position, but the person takes a complaining, blaming stance. Both these positions indicate a Child ego-state with discounting of self.

English classes Parent racketeers as either 'Helpful' or 'Bossy'. In either role, the racketeer takes a one-up stance. Again, both stances entail discounting, this time of the other person. Helpful offers the other person assistance or support while believing 'This person needs my help, because she's not capable of helping herself.' The counsellor in the imaginary example above was taking this Helpful role. Bossy criticizes or bullies the other person, believing 'This person can't get by unless I take control and boss him around.' Racketeering between Bratty and Bossy might sound like this made-up example:

CLIENT: Aw, I'm fed up! Had another row with the boss today. Just can't talk to that pig!

COUNSELLOR: *[In error]* OK! Put your boss right there on that cushion and tell him: 'Boss, you're a pig! I'm not going to take any more of this from you!'

CLIENT: *[Fidgets]* Don't think I could do that. How would it help, anyway?

COUNSELLOR: *[In error]* Just trust me! You have trust issues anyway, you know that. Now go ahead, put your boss on the cushion!

Your task in counselling is to decline each of your client's invitations into racketeering. This may demand close attention on your part, since these ulterior invitations will often sound on the social level like calls for empathy or help. To distinguish racketeering gambits from the genuine article, you can use all the techniques given in an earlier section of this chapter for detecting and confronting *discounts*. An invitation into racketeering will always entail an ulterior message (recall Chapter 1) with a discount on the psychological level.

Self-supervision 9.4

CONFRONTING RACKETEERING

Using a tape segment from a recent session, note answers to the following:

1   At what points did your client invite you into racketeering?
2   From which ego-state did he issue his invitation?
3   At each of these points, did you accept or confront?

(Continued)

(Continued)

4 If you confronted, how did your client respond?
5 If you accepted the invitation into racketeering, which ego-state did you respond from? What did you and your client do next?
6 Stroke yourself for what you did effectively this time.
7 Note anything you will do differently next time.

Confronting Games

You learned in Chapter 6 that a game typically starts like a racketeering interchange. But in a game there comes a moment when one party suddenly changes her behaviour. If she has been racketeering from a one-down stance, she shifts to one-up, and vice versa. The other person usually changes stance at the same time. This sudden change is called the Switch. It is the defining characteristic of a game. Immediately after the Switch, each player feels a moment of confusion and then takes a harvest of intense racket feelings.

A person in script typically plays out the same game sequence time and time again, with only minor details of content varying from one occasion to the next. Yet every time he plays the game and comes to the 'sickening lurch' of the Switch, he says to himself: 'This is all so familiar – but I didn't expect it to happen again!'

Once you have agreed a treatment contract with your client, your task is to confront his games each time he begins playing them in counselling sessions. You can also show him how to step out of the games he has been playing with people outside the counselling relationship.

TA writers have suggested many ingenious techniques for confronting games (for example, Berne, 1964a; Dusay, 1966; James, 1976). I sum up the principles of game confrontation in Key Ideas panel 9.2.

Key Ideas 9.2

CONFRONTING GAMES

1 To confront a game, you must interrupt its predictable flow.
2 Thus the first step in confronting a game is to become aware of the moves in that game.

3 You can then interrupt the game by intervening at *any* stage. You can do this by inviting the game-player to do *anything* other than the predictable move called for in the game. You may also shift your own response so that it does not fit the game-player's expectations.

4 Along with the interruption, you may also offer the player a non-scripty option to replace the 'expected' step in the game. This provides him with a new exit from the game sequence.

5 If your interruption is accepted, all the subsequent stages in the game will be forestalled.

In the subsections that follow, I outline some ways to confront games. In fact, with the knowledge you have gained from earlier sections of this chapter, you are already well equipped for confrontation.

Confronting the discounts

You will recall that every stage in the game entails a *discount.* Thus you can intervene effectively by using any of the techniques you know for detecting and confronting discounts (see above, this chapter). The earlier in the game you manage to pick up and deal with the discount, the more of the game you will forestall. Most effective of all is to confront the first discount, which comes in the opening ulterior transaction.

Disowning the racket-feeling payoff

You know also that the payoff of a game always entails the player experiencing racket feelings. Thus even if the person has played the game through to the payoff, you can help him defuse the game in future by inviting him to feel an authentic feeling instead of the racket feeling (see the section above on 'Confronting the myth of make-feel').

Moving into intimacy at the Switch

It is typical of games that once the player comes to the Switch, he takes it for granted that his *only possible* next step is to experience the familiar moment of confusion and move to the racket payoff. However, Emily Ruppert (1986) has pointed out that the person has a different option. Every game is a strategy that the player learned to use in childhood as a roundabout means of manipulating others to meet his needs. At the moment of the Switch, suggests Ruppert, the player can move out of the game by choosing to express his authentic need directly. Along with this will go expression of the authentic feeling that the person has previously been covering with the racket-feeling payoff. Berne (1964a) used the term *intimacy* to describe this sharing of authentic wants and feelings.

If a person takes this new exit from a game, she moves literally into 'uncharted territory'. So long as the person stayed within the scripty flow of the game, the moment of confusion after the Switch would be followed by the familiarity of the payoff. But if the person chooses intimacy instead of the payoff, she voluntarily stays with the confusion. Shifting out of the game, she also shifts out of her script. Thus she is obliged to 'go back to the drawing-board' and work out what here-and-now response she is going to make instead of the familiar scripty response.

She will not necessarily experience her new exit as more comfortable than the old game pattern. Indeed, she may feel acute discomfort at first as she struggles with new and untried options. Her satisfaction, and yours as counsellor, is that she has accepted adult responsibility for whatever outcome she now chooses.

John: Confrontation of Games

It was in this way that John broke out of his long-term game. He had already made the first move to change by coming to counselling instead of simply playing the game through to its bad-feeling pay-off. His next important step had been to close escape hatches. By doing so he had made it possible for himself in Child to give up the saving of 'anger stamps' that he had used until then to justify his game payoffs.

With the foundation laid in this way, I invited John to move out of his game into intimacy. In session fourteen, he had shared with me that he had become clearly aware how scared he was that Helen might leave him. What he wanted was that she would stay with him. I suggested that he might take a contract to tell Helen openly what he had just told me. John accepted this contract.

He went on to carry out what he had agreed. Instead of assailing Helen with racket anger, he told her he had been scared in case she would reject him. He said that what he most wanted from her was that she would stay with him.

Helen had not come into counselling herself. John reported that she responded to his openness at first with surprise and even suspicion. He had been aware that in telling her what he really felt and wanted, he was taking a risk. For all John knew, she might have decided to reject him anyway. This risk always exists when one person in a relationship chooses to move out of a game. It is not possible to 'make' the other person abandon his or her game in return. In the event, Helen did not leave John, but she took a long time to adjust to his new way of relating. She was still in this process at the time John left counselling.

In this chapter we have looked at ways in which you can invite your client to clarify and strengthen his Adult functioning. We go on in the next chapter to look at techniques you can use to invite him to make changes in Child. If he chooses to do so, he will get back in touch with the childhood experiences and decisions that have been the foundations of his life-script.

Further Reading in *Developing TA Counselling*

Points 26 and 27 in *Developing TA Counselling* (Stewart, 1996a) give more suggestions on how you can confront script effectively while maintaining rapport with your client.

10

MAKING NEW DECISIONS

The Theory of Redecision
Redecision Technique
Further Reading in *Developing TA Counselling*

You know from Chapter 3 and Chapter 6 that the life-script is based on *decisions* the person makes in childhood. When in script as an adult, she re-runs these infant strategies, though they may now have become painful or self-limiting for her. Thus the person in script is acting, thinking and feeling as she did at particular times during her childhood. That is, she is in a Child ego-state.

It thus seems reasonable to suggest that if the grown-up person wants to change these early decisions, she can do so most effectively by making her new decisions also *while in the Child ego-state*. This assumption gives the basis for the TA concept of *redecision* (Goulding and Goulding, 1972, 1976, 1978, 1979; Kadis, 1985).

Goulding (1985: 10) defines redecision as 'the decision made by the patient while in her Child ego-state to redo early decisions made by her while still an actual child.'

Robert and Mary Goulding are the originators of the redecision school in current TA. Their approach combines the cognitive framework of TA theory with affective techniques drawn from gestalt therapy (cf. Perls, 1971, 1976; Clarkson, 1989).

In the first part of this chapter I outline the theoretical rationale for redecision work. In the second part I describe the process and sequence of redecision. I suggest a selection of techniques that you can call on at each stage of this process.

The Theory of Redecision

In terms of the ego-state model, we can make a clear distinction between new decisions made in the Adult ego-state and those made in Child.

When we speak of someone making a new decision in Adult, we mean simply that he is using his grown-up resources to achieve some change that he desires in the present. This here-and-now change *may* also satisfy Child motivations that the person is holding outside of his awareness. However, it may not. Indeed, some seemingly sensible Adult changes may only serve to make matters worse from the person's perspective in Child.

Robert Goulding (1985) gives an example of this from his own experience. He reports that at one time he made a purely Adult decision to work fewer hours. Instead of the feeling of relief he might have expected, Goulding tells us he '... ended up with a huge headache. In effect, my little Kid was saying "Hey, I've been getting strokes all these years for working hard, and now I am deciding not to work hard, and I miss my strokes."'

In making a *redecision*, the person attends directly to Child motives like these. Rather than merely taking Adult control over his own patterns of scripty behaviour, he makes changes in Child that help him give up using these infant strategies altogether.

Redecision and the Racket System

The process of redecision can be related to the explanatory framework of the Racket System (Chapter 3).

You will recall that the infant is seen as making her early decisions not only by using age-appropriate thinking, but also in terms of what she does with feelings. Failing to get her needs met by the expression of an uncensored feeling, she 'explains away' her failure in the magical, concrete terms of which an infant is capable. That 'explanation', reiterated over a period of time, constitutes the script decision. The infant then represses the original feeling. To get needs met as best she can, she decides instead on a whole range of behaviours and feelings designed to extort support from her caretakers. Carried forward into adult life, these become the person's rackety displays and racket feelings. The infant's script decision, likewise carried into adulthood without awareness, becomes the grown-up person's script belief.

A central feature of redecision is that the person, while in the Child ego-state, becomes fully aware that she has ways of getting her needs met in the present that were not open to her at the time of her original early decision. This is possible because the grown-up person has resources that she did not have available when she was a young child.

As the person in Child becomes aware of the new ways in which she can get her needs met, she can begin to let go of the old manipulative strategies she decided upon as an infant. Thus she will feel less need to engage in rackety displays and to experience racket feelings. In place of those feelings, she can allow herself to experience and express the original, authentic feeling she has been repressing since the time of her script decision.

As she tests out expressing authentic feeling and using her adult powers to get needs met, she no longer has to replay her infant 'explanations' of why these needs were not met by her original caretakers. In other words, she can let go of her script beliefs. In their place she can put perceptions of self, others and the world that are based on reality-testing in the here-and-now.

Indicators of Redecision

When the person makes a redecision, he is likely to signal this by changes in the way he thinks, feels or behaves. He may change in one or more of these areas (cf. Erskine and Moursund, 1988).

- His *thinking* in the area of the redecision will now more often be based in present reality, and less often be distorted to fit his script beliefs. To say this in another way: he will spend more time thinking clearly and less time redefining and discounting.
- He will more often experience and express *authentic feelings* in place of racket feelings.
- Since he now feels less need to 'justify' those racket feelings, he will be less inclined to engage in rackety displays. Instead he will rely more on styles of *behaviour* that are designed to get his needs met directly, in ways befitting his powers as an adult.

In addition, redecision is often accompanied by changes in the person's body (Erskine, 1980; Erskine and Moursund, 1988). These may be clearly defined, as when the person reports relief from somatic discomforts such as racing pulse, excessive sweating or muscle pains. Alternatively, redecision may be signalled by a more subtle set of bodily changes. Often these are more obvious to others than to the person herself. Typically, observers will say they see her as 'softer', 'warmer', 'looking more relaxed' and so on. This reflects the fact that early decisions are often made partly in terms of held bodily patterns (Chapter 3). As the person changes the decision, she can also let go of the muscular tension that went with it.

Degrees of redecision

Redecision hardly ever takes the form of a once-off, all-or-nothing change. It is not as though the person starts from a position of being wholly committed to the script decision, then changes over to the new decision at one stroke. Instead, redecision is a matter of degree and often takes time. Any early decision may be wholly or partly redecided. The person may revisit a particular area of change several times over in counselling or therapy. Each time, she has the opportunity to strengthen a redecision she has already made in that area (Erskine, 1973; Stewart and Joines, 1987).

Further, if the person is to make the redecision a permanent part of her life, she must consistently practise the new behaviours arising from that redecision (Goulding and Goulding, 1979; Pulleyblank and McCormick, 1985). In this way also, redecision emerges not as a once-off change, but rather as a process that the person engages in over an extended period of time.

The Role of the Counsellor in Redecision

In later sections of this chapter, I shall describe techniques you can use in counselling to facilitate your clients in making redecisions. However, it is worth saying that the client can make redecisions in many other ways that do not entail the use of redecision technique. The client may make a redecision in Child while you and he are working on a purely Adult level. Sometimes the redecision will have more to do with the congruent modelling you provide than with the overt content of your counselling sessions.

For example, suppose your client made the early decision 'I Mustn't Trust'. You and he may spend a number of sessions in Adult discussion, perhaps analysing the content of his Racket System. On the basis of this, he may be busy testing out new behaviours from Adult. Yet outside of his awareness in Child, he has been just as interested in testing *you* out. Would you abandon him or play cruel tricks on him in the way he perceived his parent-figures doing when he was an infant? Gradually he develops confidence in Child that he can indeed trust you to be honest and to stay with him. This in itself constitutes the beginnings of a redecision.

When you do use redecision technique, what do you contribute to the client's process of change? First of all, you need to invite the client into her Child ego-state. Then you must find ways of facilitating her to be aware of her here-and-now, grown-up options and resources *while she is still in Child*. Finally you need to work with her as she integrates the newly decided ways of thinking, feeling and behaving into her everyday Adult functioning. The techniques described in the rest of this chapter are all designed to achieve these ends.

Redecision Technique

I begin this part of the chapter by describing the steps in treatment that must be completed if you are to lay a solid foundation for redecision. Next I give an overview of the typical sequence of redecision work. The remaining sections describe each step in that sequence in more detail.

I use a piece of redecision work with John to illustrate the sequence stage by stage.

Laying the Foundations for Redecision

Before you begin redecision work with your client, you will normally have completed all the steps in the treatment sequence that I have described in Chapters 5 to 8. In particular, there are two steps in treatment that are essential preconditions for redecision:

- The client must have closed all three escape hatches[*] (Chapter 7).
- You must have negotiated a clear contract for change (Chapter 8).

With these two steps securely completed, you and your client have a sound foundation for redecision work. Indeed, they are themselves a powerful encouragement to the client to move spontaneously to redecision.

By contrast, if you were to go ahead *without* these necessary foundations, the use of redecision technique would almost certainly be ineffective. Worse, it could potentially be harmful to the client. To remind

---

[*] As I mentioned in Chapter 7, this condition is satisfied if the client has congruently closed the hatches for a time-limited period, so long as that period has not run out.

yourself why this is so, you may wish to review the discussion of 'Tragic Script Outcomes' in Chapters 3 and 7.

Pulleyblank and McCormick (1985) stress also that before embarking on redecision work, you and your client must have built up personal rapport. The client must know you well enough to experience you in Child as safe and trustworthy. With some clients, this trust-building stage may take much longer than the redecision work that follows.

Providing a safe setting

During redecision work, it is important that the client should feel safe to express feelings openly. This feeling release may potentially be noisy or violent. Thus before you decide to use redecision technique you must ensure that the setting is safe and appropriate. Here are some points to check:

- The client should be able to make a noise without anyone outside the counselling room hearing her. At the very least, anyone who can hear her must be briefed about what is going on, and the client must know this.
- There should be plenty of large cushions for the client to pound or kick. It may be advisable to have the client sit on a cushion that in turn is placed on a mattress. Ensure that if the client does get into rage release, she is in no danger of striking hard surfaces or breakable objects.
- If you are considering starting redecision work part-way through a session, be aware of the time. It is advisable not to begin a redecision piece unless you have at least twenty minutes before the end of the session.

The Typical Sequence of Redecision Work

I have developed this 'typical sequence' from the work of Goulding and Goulding (1979), McNeel (1976) and Pulleyblank and McCormick (1985), with additional material of my own (Stewart, 1987, 1996a).

We start from the supposition that the client has closed all escape hatches and that you have negotiated an overall treatment contract. The steps in the sequence then are:

1   Establish a clear *session contract*.
2   Invite your client to *re-experience a recent scene* that exemplifies the problem he has brought to counselling. As he describes this scene, note the *racket feeling* he is experiencing. Listen for his expression of the accompanying *script beliefs*.
3   Next ask the client to *re-experience a scene from his own childhood* that relates to the recent scene he has just been describing. Check that the client is reporting the same racket feeling as in the recent scene. It is this racket feeling that forms the link between the recent scene and the early scene. Listen also for the *script decisions* that the client voices in the recalled early scene. These are the childhood counterpart of his present-day script beliefs.
4   Facilitate your client *while he is still in the Child ego-state* to become aware of the full grown-up resources he has available *in the present* for surviving and getting his needs met. This step will often flow into the next.
5   Invite the client, still in the Child ego-state, to *make a new decision* that takes full advantage of his present resources. Watch and listen for a shift out of the *racket feeling* and into *authentic feeling*, or verbal confirmation of the new decision, delivered congruently. You may also see the typical 'softening' of facial and body outline that often accompanies redecision.
6   Ask the client to return to the Adult ego-state. Invite him to '*anchor*' his redecision immediately in the here-and-now. This means asking him to engage in some behaviour, or to be aware of some sensory stimulus, that he can use on future occasions as a trigger to reactivate his experience of the redecision.
7   Carry out an *Adult de-brief*. Here you discuss with the client his Adult understanding of the new decision he has just made. It is often useful at this stage to refer back to the original session contract and check how far the client has achieved it.
8   Finally, negotiate a clear contract for new behaviours by the client that he will use to *practise* the redecision consistently.

Step 1: Establishing the Session Contract

I have already described ways in which you can invite a clear session contract (Chapter 8). You can open effectively by asking a question that looks forward to an outcome instead of backward to the problem. For example: 'What do you want to have achieved by the end of this session?'

As the client responds, listen especially for what the Gouldings call the 'first con' (Goulding and Goulding, 1979: 90). You may hear redefinitions like 'work on', 'try to', or note non-verbal incongruity. All these are signals that the client in Child may be mustering up covert defences against the perceived threat to her script beliefs.

It is crucial that you confront any such opening 'con'. Redecision sessions can often be dramatic and exciting. You may therefore feel impatient to go ahead and 'get into the work' even though you have not heard clearly from your client what change she wants to make. Do not take this route. Do not go ahead with redecision techniques until the client has said clearly, without redefining, what she wants to get from the session. In my experience, when redecision work ends up 'getting nowhere', this is almost always because the initial session contract was unclear or because the counsellor failed to confront a 'first con'.

As always, the contract statement needs to be positive and observable. The key question is: How will you and the client be able to see and hear that she has achieved her goal for the session? Stay with your client at this opening stage until you and she know the answer to this question.

Sometimes the end result may be that your fifty-minute hour runs out before you even have time to start any of the other stages of the sequence. So long as you have spent those fifty minutes in Adult discussion and appropriate confrontation, this outcome is all well and good. For this client at this time, it is likely that specifying a clear goal for change *is* the therapeutic issue.

Tracking script change during a session

Often during redecision work, the client will complete the initial session contract part-way through the session. From the content of her work at that point, you may be aware of a further move she could make immediately that you believe would assist her movement out of script. On the usual principle of contractual method, this would imply that you need to negotiate a new session contract at that point.

But in redecision work, this presents you with a special problem. At the moment when she completes the initial contract, the client is likely to be in the Child ego-state. Were you to open discussion about a new session contract, you would have to invite the client out of Child and back into

Adult. Both you and the client would be likely to experience this as a jarring interruption of the flow of the client's work in Child. Yet if you do not invite a new contract, you run the risk of 'railroading' the client. How do you solve this dilemma?

One useful tactic is to provide for the possibility at the beginning of the session. You can do this when you have agreed the session contract but before inviting the client into Child. You might say to the client: 'During this session, I may suggest to you that you say or do particular things. If it happens that at that moment you aren't willing to say or do what I suggest, I ask that you simply ignore me. Is that OK by you?' If the client says it is OK, check that she is saying so congruently.

If you are doing redecision work with a client over an extended period, you can make this a 'blanket' request covering all the client's redecision sessions. This is what I did in my work with John. Notice that the issue at stake is what the client is *willing* to do. This may or may not be the same as what he *wants* to do.

Contracting for the unknown change

Sometimes you do not know for sure, before the client gets into the work, *what* script decision lies at the root of some present-day discomfort. You can expect that the decision may emerge as the client revisits some early scene or 'talks to' some parental figure in imagination. But how can your client take a contract to change this decision when he does not know in advance what the decision is?

There is a form of words that takes care of this possibility. First, you ask the client if he is willing to go ahead with one of the typical procedures of redecision work. Examples:

'Are you willing to go back in your imagination and re-experience a scene from your childhood, that is connected in some way to the painful scene you've just been describing to me?'

Or:

'Will you put your mother on that other cushion in imagination, and express to her how you feel about her not wanting you to exist?'

As always, check whether a 'Yes' response is given congruently. If it is, go on to ask an if-question: 'And if, in the course of this work, you become aware of a childhood decision you made that is now limiting or painful for you, are you willing to change that decision for a new one that takes account of your full resources as a grown-up person?'

This emphasizes yet again how important it is for the client to have closed escape hatches before beginning redecision work. Were the hatches not closed, it could be hazardous for the client to accept a blanket contract to change *any* early decision.

Step 2: Re-experiencing a Recent Scene

This second step is not applicable to all pieces of redecision work. Where you and the client have already agreed a strategy of moves toward some specified script change, you may move directly from establishing the session contract (step 1) straight into some redecision procedure such as chairwork (see step 3).

However, the client may often begin a session by stating a vaguely defined desire for change, or by referring in general terms to the problem he has brought to counselling. In these circumstances it is useful to invite him to re-experience a specific scene from his current life that exemplifies the problem or the perceived need for change. Notice that you ask the client to *re-experience* the scene, not just to 'talk about' it.

Mary and Robert Goulding (1979) suggest a brief sequence of interventions to achieve this purpose. Suppose the client has opened with a statement of a general problem or a vaguely phrased wish for change. You then ask 'Will you give me a recent example of this?'

When the client begins to describe a recent scene, say 'Now, if you will, *be* there. Will you tell it in the present, as though the scene is happening now?'

After a few sentences, the client may slip back into using the past tense. If so, simply invite him back into describing the scene in the present tense, and imagining himself in the scene as he speaks.

Where the recent scene entailed some interaction with another person, you may invite the client to 'put' the other person on an empty chair in imagination, and re-enact the conversation. Ask him to take his own part alternately with that of the other person, changing chairs as he switches from one identity to the other.

As he re-experiences the recent scene the client may already shift into the Child ego-state, even though the scene he is experiencing is one from his adult life. You are likely to hear him expressing the same racket feeling, and voicing the same script beliefs, as he did in the recent scene itself. You may assist the process by asking: 'So at the end of all this, how do you feel? And what are you saying in your head about yourself? About other people? About life generally?' As always, wait for the answer to one question before you ask the next.

Using the recent scene in contract-making

Where the client has begun by stating a vaguely defined wish for change, you may find it useful to reverse the order of steps 1 and 2 in the sequence. This allows you to use the client's experience of the recent scene to help establish a clear contract for change in the session. You first invite the client back to the recent scene in the way I have described above. Then you ask:

'So in this scene, what is it you need to do differently so as to get a result that's pleasant for you instead of painful?'

You can invite the client to 'stay in' the scene and build up a detailed visualization of how he and others see and hear him behaving in the new way. The client now has a clearly defined goal for behavioural change. Later, at the end of the redecision session, you can return to this goal and ask if he is willing to go ahead in reality and perform the behaviour he has just been visualizing.

'The others are not to be changed'

Notice that you invite the client to visualize how *he* can behave differently to achieve the outcome he wants. You do not ask him to imagine a scene in which *others* behave differently from the way they actually behaved in the scene itself. This principle is crucial to all stages of redecision work. Mary and Robert Goulding (1979: 206) sum it up in the directive:

* 'The others are *not* to be changed.'

John: Steps 1 and 2

The piece of work that I am using as illustration comes from session fifteen. John and I had already agreed on the overall change that he wanted to achieve. He wanted to cease his habitual pattern of getting violent with his girlfriends. Instead, he wanted to find ways of being open about his feelings and asking directly for what he wanted.

I asked him to recall a recent situation where he had got aggressive with his girlfriend. John named an occasion a few weeks before when he had felt bad because it seemed to him Helen was offering him no affection. Instead of asking for what he wanted from her, he had snapped at her. She had responded by withdrawing from him. Eventually he had yelled at her and stormed out of the house.

I asked him to put Helen on another cushion in imagination and re-run their interaction, taking both parts in turn. John agreed. This was our opening session contract.

As he spoke with 'Helen', John said to her: 'I don't *want* to quarrel with you like this all the time. But I just find myself doing it again. I don't know how I can help it.'

He didn't want to, but he did again and again. I picked up the conflict and used it as a key into step 3 of the sequence.

Step 3: Re-experiencing the Related Early Scene

In this third step, you have a delicate task. You need to invite your client to 'go back' to her childhood and re-experience a situation that is likely to have been painful for her. Yet if this experience is to be therapeutic, she must also remain aware of here-and-now reality. In ego-state terms, she must keep some energy in Adult functioning even while she is accessing Child script memories.

Why is this essential? Because the central feature of redecision is that the client gets in touch with her *present* resources while re-experiencing a *past* scene. In order to have access to those present resources, she needs to retain her awareness of the present.

Were the client to shift entirely into Child, temporarily abandoning all Adult functioning, she would merely re-run the remembered painful experience. Since she would not be introducing new resources, the outcome of the scene would be the same as it was in the client's childhood. The result would be anti-therapeutic: she would simply add the unchanged scene to her store of reinforcing memories.

Transactional analysts have devised various techniques to achieve the therapeutic goals of step 3. I shall describe two that are widely used:

- early-scene work
- chairwork.

Early-scene work

As its name implies, early-scene work means inviting the client to re-experience a scene from childhood. This scene will in some way be a counterpart to the painful situation reported in the client's current life.

Notice that even in early-scene work, you and the client are not actually 'working with the past'. It is impossible to work in the past. What you are doing instead is to help the client experience his *present* memory of a past scene. The past scene itself can no longer be changed. But the client can change his *present experience* of that scene by introducing into it the resources and options he has available as an adult. This in turn helps him change his responses to similar actual situations in the present.

To initiate early-scene work, one approach is simply to ask the client 'Does all this remind you of anything from your childhood?' If he does call up a memory, you can go straight ahead by asking him to 'be there' and speak in the present, as you did for the recent scene.

An alternative is to trace memories back from the recent scene, through scenes that reach further and further back into the client's past. The linking factor in all these scenes is the *racket feeling* that the client experienced. Thus when the client has described his experience of the recent scene in step 2, you might ask: 'So at the end of all this, you felt *(name the racket feeling)*. Will you go back now in your memory to a time about a year ago, and recall a scene where you ended up feeling the same way?'

When the client recalls such a scene, ask him to describe it briefly, using the present tense as usual. Once he has done so, ask him to put that scene aside for now. Repeat your first question, but this time ask for a scene from, say, five years back in which he felt the same racket feeling.

Trace back in this way to earlier and earlier scenes. Usually the client will be able to make connections back to scenes in his childhood. Eventually he will say he cannot recall an earlier scene. When he does so, continue to work with the earliest scene he has recalled.

Most transactional analysts agree that the early scene so recalled is likely to represent a 'screen memory'. That is, you are likely to work with a scene from the client's middle or late childhood rather than from infancy. This is probably not the scene in which the client in fact began making the script decision in question. It is more likely to have been an occasion on which he consolidated a decision that he had begun making earlier in his childhood. However, experience suggests that working with the screen memory can be effective as a means of changing the script decision.

Sometimes a client will have blanked out all or most memories of her childhood. She may report that she cannot recall any scene earlier than, say, teenage. In this case, you can invite her simply to make up the early scene that she *would* have recalled if she had been able to recall it. Then go ahead and work with the fantasized scene.

Chairwork

As you worked with the recent scene at step 2, you may already have invited your client to put himself on one chair and 'talk with' an imagined person on the other chair. If so, you have already begun chairwork. Now you have various options for shifting to step 3.

(a) You may simply ask your client whether this exchange reminds him of anything from his childhood (for example, a remembered conversation with his mother or father). If he says it does, invite him to put the figure from childhood on the other chair and talk with him or her.

(b) Alternatively, you can invite your client to 'take off the mask'. As he continues to speak to the person on the other cushion, listen for a shift into the racket feeling. At that point, say to the client: 'Look across now at *(name the other person)*. As you do that, you realize that the person you are looking at is really someone else, wearing a mask with *(name)*'s face on it. If you will, reach across now and take off the mask. *(Wait for the client to do this)* Now, whose face do you see behind that mask?'

The face seen will often be that of a parent-figure. Sometimes the client will see his own face. He may see the face of some symbolic figure. The face to work with is the one he sees first.

(c) If you have not already initiated chairwork at step 2, you may do so now at step 3. Listen for any *conflict* the client is expressing in the recent scene. For example:

> 'I'm so tired of overworking, but I can't seem to stop it.'
> 'I do want to talk to my husband about how I feel. But somehow I can't find the words.'

'It's the same old thing. I diet for a while, lose weight really well, then binge and put it all back on again.'

Invite the client to divide the sides of the conflict between two chairs. Then ask him to 'be' each side in turn and talk for himself, using 'I'. In the first example above, you might ask him to sit in one chair and 'be' the side of himself that is tired of overworking. In the second chair he would 'be' the part of himself that continues to work hard nevertheless.

(d) Sometimes, particularly when your client is familiar with redecision work, she may already know that she wants to 'speak to' a specific parent or parent-figure on the other chair. In that case, your response will usually be to accept that contract and invite her to go ahead with the two-chair conversation (provided that it makes sense to you as a way of furthering the client's script change).

Impasses

Whether in an early scene or in chairwork, the client by this point has entered in fantasy into a two-sided interchange. One side will initially be experienced as 'self', the other side as 'not self'.

In early-scene work, 'self' will be the client as a child. 'Not self' will usually be a parent or other figure perceived as having had power over the person in childhood. In two-chair work, 'self' and 'other' will be the two divided sides of the conflict. Typically, as the conversation proceeds, 'self' will emerge as a Child ego-state, while 'other' turns out to be Parent.

Almost always, 'self' will begin by taking a one-down position in the exchange. The 'other' will be experienced as one-up. 'Self' will be needy, lost, downtrodden, deprived, petulant and so on. 'Other' may be bossy, cruel, smothering, tyrannical or heartless (McNeel, 1976).

In this situation, it frequently happens that the client feels stuck in a conflict between 'self' and 'other'. This 'stuck point' is known as an *impasse* (Goulding and Goulding, 1979; cf. Perls, 1971, 1976). In current TA theory, every impasse is modelled as an intrapsychic conflict between a Parent and a Child part of the client's ego-state structure (Mellor, 1980a). In the client's internal dialogue, the Parent repeats a *script message* (recall Chapter 6) – for example, 'Don't Be You'. The Child responds with an autonomous want for change – in this example, 'I want to be me!' Each side in the internal conflict pushes with equal force, with the result that the client expends a lot of energy but stays stuck in the script.

In two-chair work, it is usually obvious that an impasse entails conflict, because the two sides in the conversation get embroiled in an argument or because one side makes demands that the other side refuses to fulfil. When an impasse arises in early-scene work, the conflictual element is sometimes not so immediately apparent, but always exists: the child in the early scene wants to do or say something, but does not, because she believes that to do so would be met by a negative response – wrath, physical harm, ridicule, abandonment – from some powerful (Parental) figure.

Impasses are classified as *Type 1, Type 2* and *Type 3*. The three types refer to three different developmental stages in childhood at which the relevant script decisions were made; the issues in the internal conflict are those which typically arise for the child at that stage of development. Each type of impasse relates to a particular component of the script, again according to the developmental stage at which that aspect of the script was decided by the child. (You may find it helpful at this point to refer back to Chapter 6's description of life-script, particularly the distinction between the *counterscript* and the *script proper*). In summary:

- A *Type 1 impasse* is a conflict around script decisions made in later childhood, when the child has coherent command of language. Thus the issues arising in a Type 1 impasse will relate to the *counterscript*. The struggles here will be about what the child ought or ought not to do, what kinds of behaviour are viewed as socially acceptable or unacceptable.
- In a *Type 2 impasse,* the script decisions in question are those made in early childhood, when the child has only rudimentary use of language. We are thus referring to the decisions that make up the *script proper*. The content of the conflict here will typically turn on the Gouldings' twelve script themes (Goulding and Goulding, 1976), described above in Chapter 6: for example, is the child to stay alive or drop dead? Be herself or somebody else? Be important or unimportant?
- The conflicts that typify a *Type 3 impasse* are those which arise for the infant, at a stage of development that pre-dates even the script proper.[*] This infant will have virtually no command of language. The issues arising in the conflict will reflect the developmental struggles that

---

[*] Eric Berne made only brief reference to this very early stage in the formation of the script, calling it the *protocol* (Berne, 1961: 118). Since Berne's time, TA has learned a great deal from object-relations theory about the importance of these early developmental tasks. The references given in the text will give you a good starting-point if you would like to follow this topic up further.

every infant must face: for example, abandonment vs. engulfment; annihilation vs. being annihilated; worth vs. worthlessness; basic trust vs. basic mistrust (Cornell and Landaiche, 2006; Erikson, 1950; Gobes, 1985; Haykin, 1980; Klein, 1987).

Recognizing the three types of impasse

By what practical clues do you distinguish the three types of impasse one from another? Here are some guidelines:

- *Type 1 impasse*   In a Type 1 exchange, the Parent gives out script messages in response to which the child decided his *counterscript*. Thus on the Parent side of the conversation you will typically hear slogans like:

  'Big boys don't cry.'
  'You've made your bed, now you have to lie in it.'
  'Only the best is good enough.'
  'If at first you don't succeed, try, try, try again.'

  'Self', as Child, either complies glumly with these commands or rebels petulantly against them.
- *Type 2 impasse*   Here, the fantasized Parent will express the harsher, more punitive script messages the person will have perceived in earlier childhood when she was deciding upon the *script proper*. You may hear:

  'I wish I'd never had you!'
  'I'll kill you for that.'
  'Just you shut your mouth and don't be so damn smart.'

  'Self' is likely to show behavioural clues appropriate to an earlier developmental stage of the Child than in the Type 1 impasse. Instead of being compliant or bratty, this Child may feel unwanted, cornered, enraged or despairing.
- *Type 3 impasse*   In work with a Type 3 impasse, especially when it is done with little use of langue, it may be difficult to distinguish at first which side of the conflict represents Parent and which represents Child. The 'other' in Type 3 work often represents some aspect of personality that the client has been disowning, or that he feels to be threatening. This 'other' may often be portrayed in symbolic ways that have their roots in the infant's magical thinking. 'Self' may end up talking in imagination to the Devil, to a ferocious wolf, to a damp grey

cloud of sadness, or to the pain he has been feeling in his back. Despite the apparently threatening or lethal nature of such symbolic figures, they always have a positive intention for the client (Mellor, 1980a; Stewart, 1996a: 190–1, 200–4). Often, this positive intention entails some kind of control: for example, a pain in the back turns out to have the positive intention of stopping the client working too hard. Formally in the theory of impasses, the entity experienced as 'other' is modelled as Parent, while 'self' is modelled as Child.

Whichever of these ego-state conflicts your client shows, your task now is to help her resolve it. She can achieve this by getting in touch with her here-and-now resources and deciding to use them.

The process of impasse resolution can be summarized as follows. First, the client contacts her ability to survive without the internal parent. Aware now in Child that she does not need to 'keep the parent around', she next breaks free from some parental constraint that she has been imposing upon herself. At any point in this process the client may engage in feeling release, as she lets go of the racket feeling and encounters the authentic feeling that has been hidden beneath it. Finally, the client achieves reconciliation with the internal parent. These stages will not necessarily all be completed in one session. In the next section, I shall give transcripts to illustrate various practical techniques that you can use to help your client break out of impasses and move to redecision. (If you would like to read more extended transcripts of redecision technique in action, you can find them in Goulding and Goulding, 1979, and in Joines and Stewart, 2002). Resolution of a Type 3 impasse may take place in the way you would intuitively expect: with a great deal of physical release (beating cushions, screaming, vomiting) and little or no use of language. When the impasse is resolved in this kind of Type 3 work, the effect for the client is usually physical rather than cognitive: she may experience release or relaxation, and often feels like going to sleep. However, there is another style of Type 3 resolution that sounds quite different, but is equally valid for the client. Here, the two conflicted sides of the impasse get down to negotiation, using language in a way that may appear to be Adult. There may be no obvious feeling release. Closure is achieved when the two parties have negotiated a clear behavioural compromise that at least satisfies the wants of each.

When the client resolves a Type 1 impasse, be alert for the possibility that she may encounter a Type 2 or Type 3 impasse immediately or shortly afterwards (Goulding, 1977). This is likely to occur if she has been using her counterscript belief to defend against a belief from the script proper (recall Chapter 6, section on *The Dynamics of the Script*). As the client resolves the Type 1 impasse, she lets go of the counterscript belief. In so doing she uncovers the belief from the script proper, hence moves into the Type 2 or Type 3 impasse.

John: Step 3

In re-telling his recent scene, John had voiced a conflict. I thus asked him now if he would put on one cushion the part of himself that had kept on picking quarrels with Helen. On the other cushion I invited him to put the part that wanted to stop being aggressive and instead be open about his needs. He did so and opened a conversation between the parts.

I was not certain at this point what script belief might be at the root of John's difficulty. Thus I asked if he would take a 'contract for the unknown change' (see above). He agreed that if he became aware of any childhood decision that was now self-limiting or painful for him, he would change it for a new decision. This was now our session contract.

John experienced his 'quarrelling part' as 'other'. Without any intervention from me, he quickly identified the 'quarrelling part' as his hectoring, violent father. He put 'father' on the other cushion and continued the conversation.

He then moved into an exchange that is typical of this stage of redecision work (McNeel, 1976). As 'himself', John was Child. He voiced demands for his 'father' to let him alone, to go away and let him do his own thing. But he made these demands from an ineffec-tual, one-down position. As John did this, he re-ran in the session the same racket feeling of petulant resentment as he had been show-ing in his recent relationship with his girlfriend. Meantime, 'father' scoffed at John from one-up Parent. The entire exchange was a replay of the way John had been 'stuck' in his childhood relation-ship with his father. Now as a grown-up, he was still sticking him-self in the same way with the 'father' in his head.

At this stage it was not clear to me which type of impasse was at issue. My guess was that the present exchange pointed to Type 1, but that a Type 2 impasse might lie below it.

Step 4: Bringing in Present Resources

At step 4, two main principles apply:

* The client needs to bring *her own* present resources into the exchange, not to borrow *your* resources.
* She needs to stay in the Child ego-state. At the same time she must retain Adult awareness.

Inviting the client's own resources

When you are closely involved in redecision work, there is often a temptation to 'help the client along' when he or she seems to be on the verge of a new decision but is not quite making it.

In the work I was doing with John, he reached such a point. He was talking in fantasy with his domineering 'father':

JOHN: [*Petulantly*] Get off my back, Dad! Why don't you just get off my back?

The temptation for me was to come in with something like this:

COUNSELLOR: [*In error*] OK, so just throw him right off! [*Gives client a cushion*] Fling him in the corner! Go on, get him off your back now. [*Client throws the cushion*] Well done!

In this made-up example, the counsellor would be *leading* the client into a new response. This kind of intervention can mean high drama in the counselling room. Both counsellor and client may feel that the client has made a genuine change.

And, in a sense, the change is genuine. The client has made a new response to the oppression of his internal 'father'. Yet the impetus for that change has come mainly from the counsellor, rather than from the client himself. As he breaks free from adaptation to his father, the client adapts to the counsellor instead. Thus he is likely to be able to maintain the change only so long as he can keep the counsellor around. He may manage this for a time, either in reality or by internalizing the counsellor as a replacement Parent. But if he loses the counsellor, he may well also lose the change.

Whenever you 'lead' the client during redecision work, you increase the risk of his adapting to you in this way. To help avoid this, you can use two practical guidelines:

1   In redecision work, *follow* a fraction of a second behind the client rather than leading.
2   Stay keenly aware of the client's 'Martian'. Watch out for non-verbal clues that indicate he may be adapting to you or rebelling against you.

Suppose then that you follow the client, and you and he come to a point at which he 'gets stuck'. It is the *client's* job to get unstuck if he chooses to do so, not your job to unstick him. So what contribution do you make at this point? You may do either or both of two things:

• Invite him to be fully aware of his stuckness.
• Invite him to be aware of the reality of his present resources.

Detailed below are some interventions you can use for these purposes.

Using 'heighteners'

A 'heightener' is an intervention that invites the client to heighten her awareness of staying stuck (McNeel, 1976). In my work with John, here is how I used heighteners:

JOHN: [*Petulantly*] Get off my back, Dad! Why don't you just get off my back?
COUNSELLOR: [*Gets a heavy cushion, places it on the client's shoulders*] OK, there he is on your back. Feel his weight.
JOHN: [*Weak voice*] Yeah, you're so heavy, Dad. I'm really, really tired of you weighing down on me.
COUNSELLOR: So feel how very tired you are. Go ahead and really droop down. Now test saying to Dad: 'Dad, I'm utterly weak and helpless. There's no way I'll ever be able get you off my back.'

With heighteners like these you are asking the client to escalate his usual scripty response. The hope is that he will become so uncomfortable in the old pattern that he spontaneously breaks out of it. John and I continued our exchange in this way:

JOHN: [*To 'father'*] Dad, I'm utterly weak and helpless. There's no way … Bloody hell, this is ridiculous! [*Bursts out laughing. Pulls the cushion off his back and drops it on the floor in front of him. Straightens up*]

COUNSELLOR: Looks like you got him off. What are you laughing at?

JOHN: Well, there I was sitting drooping. And all I had to do was reach up and lift him off.

COUNSELLOR: So test saying to him: 'Dad, I'm strong enough to get you off my back.'

JOHN: [To 'father'; strong voice] Dad, I am strong enough to get you off my back.

COUNSELLOR: True? [This query is useful as a check for congruency when you have prompted the client to say something]

JOHN: Yeah, true.

Another heightener that is often effective is the 'how long will you wait?' gambit. Often when a person is in script, he is waiting for someone else to change in the past (Goulding and Goulding, 1979). The magical Child belief is that if the person just stays sad enough, or resentful enough, or helpless enough, then the other figure from the past will eventually change and be as the client wanted him to be in childhood. The heightener makes use of this. Here is an example from the work of another client, Margery:

MARGERY: [To 'mother'] Mother, I feel really bitter about the way you treated my brother and me when we were little.

COUNSELLOR: 'And I'm going to go on feeling bitter until …'?

MARGERY: I think I'll always feel bitter at you.

COUNSELLOR: So tell her: 'Mother, I'm going to go on feeling bitter at you for the rest of my life.'

MARGERY: Yes. I think I will feel bitter at you all my life for what you did. [She is still in the racket feeling. The counsellor therefore escalates]

COUNSELLOR: So say to her: 'Mother, I'm going to keep on feeling bitter at you for the rest of my life, even though you're dead.'

MARGERY: [Pause. Holds breath]

COUNSELLOR: Breathe.

MARGERY: [Takes a breath. Begins to cry]

COUNSELLOR: [Pause] So, when you're ready, say what you want to say to your mother now.

MARGERY: [Crying] Yes, you're dead. You never showed you loved me when you were alive. I'm so sad we missed the chance.

The client has moved out of racket bitterness into authentic sadness. At the same time she has given up her waiting game. The counsellor might go on to invite her to be aware of her ability in the here-and-now to ask others for the love she had been waiting to get from her mother.

There is never any guarantee that a heightener will work. Sometimes the client will stay with his racket feeling despite every escalation you can think of. In that case your best option is probably to cease the redecision sequence and invite him back into Adult. If you are taping the session, you may play the tape back to him and ask him to be aware of the way he is choosing to stay with his old strategy. You may also review his possible Child motivations for staying stuck.

Inviting awareness of resources

Your aim is to invite the client to be aware of his present resources while he remains in Child. Clearly it would *not* be a good idea, when your client is in the middle of a Child scene, to intervene with something like: 'So just pause a minute, and think how you're different as a grown-up nowadays from how you were back then as a kid.'

Instead you have to find some way of asking the client to be aware of the reality of his present options while still re-experiencing the past scene. One way of doing this is to invite him to 'stay the age he is' in the imagined scene, and at the same time give himself the knowledge, experience, and so on that he has as his grown-up self. A typical intervention in early-scene work would be:

> COUNSELLOR: So, David, Mummy and Daddy are hitting each other and you're feeling very, very lost and scared. Now keep on being six-year-old David, and watch Mummy and Daddy as they fight. And while you do that, give yourself grown-up David's understanding and grown-up David's knowledge of people. [*Pause*] Now do you say anything different to yourself in your head?

You can also ask the client to behave in some way that invites awareness of his grown-up size and strength. While in script, he is likely to have been imagining himself as still being the size of a child.

I used this approach a few minutes further into my session with John. After getting his 'father' on to the floor in front of him, he had quite suddenly begun feeling panic-stricken. I asked him to tell 'father' how he felt:

> JOHN: [*To 'father'; shaky voice*] Dad, I can't tell you you were wrong. I'm so scared you'll hit me, scared you'll hurt me.
> COUNSELLOR: So keep him there on the cushion. Will you stand up? [*John does so*] Now look down at him. Will you show me how high on you the top of his head comes? Show me with your hand. [*John indicates a point about*

waist-height] So as you stand up and look down at him there, is there anything different you want to say to him?

JOHN: [*Pause*] I'm taller than you are, Dad. [*Quietly*] You can't hurt me now.

COUNSELLOR: Tell him that again.

JOHN: [*Stronger voice*] You can't hurt me now, Dad. No, you really can't.

Step 5: Stating the Redecision

When the client is ready, you should invite her to make a clear positive statement of whatever new decision she is making. She needs to remain in the Child ego-state as she does so.

Usually this step will flow on from step 4 without a break. Here is how this went in the piece of work with John:

COUNSELLOR: So you used your strength and got Dad off your back. And you're quite right, he can't hurt you any more now. So, if there's anything you want to say to Dad now, go ahead and say it.

JOHN: [*To 'father'*] Dad, I feel I've been carrying you around with me for so long. But I don't have to be the same as you.

COUNSELLOR: Test saying to him:'I can be different from you, Dad.' [*Invites shift from negative to positive wording: no change in meaning*]

JOHN: I can be different from you, Dad. Yes, I can be.

COUNSELLOR: True?

JOHN: Yes, that's true.

COUNSELLOR: So will you tell him how you can be different from him?

JOHN: [*To 'father'*] Dad, the only way you knew to get what you wanted from other people was to shout at them, or hit them, or get nasty. It wasn't your fault. You just didn't know any other way.

COUNSELLOR: So tell him if you know any other way.

JOHN: Yes. I can ask people for what I want.

COUNSELLOR: Test saying to Dad: 'Dad, I will ask people for what I want.' [*Explores client's willingness to shift from 'can' to 'will'*]

JOHN: [*Strong voice*] Dad, I'll ask people for what I want from them when I want it. I don't need to pick fights with people any more.

COUNSELLOR: Give yourself time to find out if what you've said is true for you. [*Pause*] Is it true?

JOHN: Yes. It's true.

COUNSELLOR: How do you feel?

JOHN: Relieved! [*Smiles and relaxes posture*]

COUNSELLOR: I'm not surprised you feel relieved. Nice work.

Watching for the 'last con'

In making the session contract, you looked out for and confronted any 'first con'. Now in the closing stages of the sequence, you need to be equally alert for a 'last con'. In Child, the client may both welcome his own new decision and be scared of its consequences. Outside of awareness, he may deal with his scare by seeking to slide out of the new decision he is apparently taking.

The possible clues to this are the same as for the 'first con'. Non-verbal let-outs are especially common at this stage. As you and the client ride on the good feeling that typically accompanies the resolution of a redecision piece, it is particularly tempting to ignore some signal that may indicate a closing con. You therefore need to be all the more vigilant. As always, check that the client delivers his statements congruently. If you observe any sign that he may be discounting or redefining, confront.

Closing the Child work

Working in Child requires a good deal of energy on the part of the client. It is therefore important to keep any one session of Child work relatively short. As a rule of thumb, close after no more than twenty minutes. If the client makes a clear redecision before then, come out earlier. You may be tempted to stay in the work, going for 'just that bit more' in the way of change for the client. It is wise not to do this. Instead, invite the client to close and celebrate the change she *has* made. You and she can always return and do more another day if you both want to. If you stay in the work until the client has run out of energy, you increase the risk that she will act on her Child fear of change and find some way of subverting the new decision.

If the client has not made a new decision in about twenty minutes, come out of the work anyway. There will be a reason why she is not ready in Child to change her decision. When she is back in Adult, you can discuss with her how she kept herself from changing. This Adult analysis may help her give herself the basis for a change in Child at some later time.

Clearing projections

Before you invite the client back into Adult, it is important that you ask him to clear away the symbolic people and things he has been imagining during the Child work.

If he has been in an early scene, check if there is anything more he wants to say to anybody in that scene before he leaves it. When he is ready, invite him to 'come back to the room'. You may ask him to look around, pick out one object in the room and describe it to you.

If you have been using chairwork, you *must* ensure that the client has the chance to remove the 'other person' he has been imagining in the room. A typical sequence would be the one I used in the work with John. You will remember that he had stated his new decision and told me he felt relieved. After stroking him for the change, I went on:

COUNSELLOR: So is there anything else you want to say to Dad before you take him off the cushion?

JOHN: Yes. [*To 'father'*] It really wasn't your fault, Dad. I wish we could have known each other better. But we didn't, and that's just how it was.

COUNSELLOR: Any more? [*This is a useful all-purpose check question*]

JOHN: Goodbye, Dad.

COUNSELLOR: Are you ready to take him off now?

JOHN: [*To counsellor*] Yes.

COUNSELLOR: OK. Go ahead and take him off the cushion. When you've got him off, will you signal you've done that by lifting the cushion and putting it behind you?

JOHN: [*does so*].

Step 6: Anchoring the Redecision

This step applies only when the client has clearly stated a redecision in step 5. As the client closes the Child work, you invite him back into Adult. Immediately he has shifted ego-state, you ask him to engage in some behaviour, or be aware of some sensory stimulus, that he can use as a link between his Adult functioning and his new Child decision.

This step need only take a few moments. An effective way is to ask the client to state to you whatever new decision he has just stated to the imagined 'other'. Continuing the example from John's work:

COUNSELLOR: [*Looks John in the eye*] Hi. Are you completely back talking to me now?

JOHN: [*Returns gaze*] Hello. Yes, I am.

COUNSELLOR: When you were imagining Dad on the other cushion, you said to him that when you wanted something from other people, you'd ask for it and that you didn't feel you needed to pick fights any more. [*John nods*] Will you find out whether you can say the same thing to me now, and mean it? [*Pause*] If you can say that and mean it, will you go ahead and say it to me now?

JOHN: Yes, I mean it. I can ask people for what I want, and I don't need to pick fights with them to get it. [*He has substituted 'can' for 'will'. I investigate whether this may be a 'closing con'*]

COUNSELLOR: Yes, you 'can' ask people for what you want. Are you going to?

JOHN: [*Laughs*] Yes, I can, and yes, I'm going to. [*His laugh was followed by a congruent statement of the new decision, not by a discount. I therefore judge that it was not a gallows laugh*]

COUNSELLOR: Great!

Step 7: Adult De-brief

This de-brief is an Adult discussion of the change that the client has just achieved. Its purpose is to provide a framework of understanding for the client's feeling work. This reflects redecision therapists' assumption that a combination of cognitive and affective work is the most effective basis for lasting change.

If you have chosen to use TA concepts explicitly in your work with the client, you may bring them into the de-brief. For example, you might draw up your initial picture of the client's Racket System. You and she could then discuss which script beliefs she had updated. From this starting point you might trace the other changes this would imply for the other parts of the system as a whole.

You may carry out the Adult debrief immediately after the client has anchored the redecision. Alternatively you can leave it for another time. As always, you and the client will make this choice between you in contractual style.

With some clients, you may have done a good deal of cognitive work in earlier sessions. If so, the debrief may only need to be a passing reference back to what you have already discussed. This was so in my work with John. By the time we began redecision work, we had already reviewed the content of his Racket System in detail. Thus we simply needed to register now what part of his old scenario he had redecided. In the piece of work he had just done, John had let go of a compound script belief that had been modelled for him by his father. That belief had been:

'I mustn't get close to anyone. And if I were to ask others openly for what I want, that would amount to getting close to them. So to get what I want, the only thing I can do is get aggressive.'

Re-checking the session contract

The debrief is also a good opportunity to review your session contract and check how far it has been fulfilled. In the example from John's work, the session contract had been that he would update any childhood decision that was now self-limiting for him. He and I agreed that he had done so.

Step 8: Contracting for New Behaviour

When the client redecides in a session, both he and you may experience this as a dramatic change. And so it is. Yet the statement of the new decision is only the door into change. If the client is to *integrate* the redecision, to make it a lasting part of his life, he needs to practise new behaviours consistent with his new decision. He may well feel awkward at first with these new ways of behaving. He may need to use determination and work hard for a time to stay with his new patterns. With practice, they will become easier.

Experience has shown that without this consistent practice, there is a considerable chance that the person may slip back into his old scripty strategies. No matter how powerful the redecision work, the person in Child will always have some motivation to return to script. This is especially the case when others to whom he relates have not changed with him. His spouse or family members may have their own Child investment in inviting him back to familiar patterns.

The final step in the redecision sequence, therefore, is for the client to take a firm contract for the behavioural change he will use to practise the redecision. From Chapter 8, you already know what is required for the negotiation of an effective contract.

If you moved into step 2 of the redecision sequence by asking the client to visualize how he might change his behaviour in a recent scene, you can return to this now and ask if he will take a contract to carry out the behaviour in reality.

In the example of my work with John, he had started by saying he wanted to break his habitual pattern of getting aggressive with women. His goal instead was to ask openly for what he wanted. This gave us a key to the behavioural contract that he might use to practise his redecision. It was obvious that Helen was one person with whom he could test out his new behaviours. The eventual form of the behavioural contract was:

'Three times in the coming week, I will ask Helen openly for something I want from her. No matter how she may respond, I will keep to my decision not to use physical violence against her or against myself. I will report to you at our next session.'

John and I registered that he would fulfil the contract by *asking* for three things, whether or not Helen agreed to do them. At the next session, he reported that he had carried out the contract. He said he was going to repeat this behaviour in successive weeks.

If you and your client agree to do so, you can use the redecision sequence for further changes she wants to make. For each of these changes, it is important that she also takes a behavioural contract to practise the new decision over a period of time. This is necessary if she is to integrate the redecision fully into her life.

Eventually the time will come when you will want to consider between you when to end counselling. This is the topic of the next and final chapter.

Further Reading in *Developing TA Counselling*

Point 29 in *Developing TA Counselling* (Stewart, 1996a) describes an alternative method for impasse resolution, based on a technique from NLP (neuro-linguistic programming). Point 30 offers some hints on how to make effective closure after redecision work.

11

ENDING COUNSELLING

Contractual Method for Termination
Criteria for Termination

Eric Berne repeatedly urged that the goal of the TA practitioner should be to *cure* the client. Yet in counselling there is no end-point that clearly corresponds to the 'cure' of a physical illness. So how can you and your client judge when to end your work together?

The *Transactional Analysis Journal* some years ago devoted an entire issue to a symposium on the concept of cure (*TAJ*, 1980). There were as many different criteria of cure as there were contributors. Berne himself gave several different accounts of cure at different points in his writings (Stewart, 1992: 79–85; cf. Clarkson, 1992: 27–39).

I shall outline three writers' views on 'cure' in the sections that follow, without suggesting that one view is better than another. There is one fixed point among all these differing opinions. That is: termination is a matter for *contractual* agreement between you and your client.

Contractual Method for Termination

Contractual method applies to termination just as it does to earlier stages of treatment in TA. Neither you nor your client has sole say in when you conclude your counselling relationship. Instead you negotiate to decide a time and manner of finishing. If you reach mutual agreement and both signify your willingness from Adult, then you have a contract for termination.

In fact, you and your client will already have agreed most of the important provisions for termination at the *beginning* of counselling. You did so in the course of negotiating your business contract (recall Chapter 5). At this initial stage you will have stated any rules on termination you wished to set as a precondition for working with the client. These will have included arrangements for what is to happen in the event of premature termination by either party. You will also have agreed an initial number of sessions. You probably specified that the last of these sessions would be given over to a review of results, and that you and your client would then agree either on further sessions or on termination.

Follow-up

There is no standard practice in TA regarding the use of a follow-up interview. My own preference is to have no follow-up, but instead to finish all there is to finish before termination. I believe that if you fix a follow-up, you run the risk that the client in Child may perceive you as issuing messages like 'Our goodbye is no goodbye at all', or 'You have to come back just in case we haven't got things perfect.'

At the same time I make clear to the client that 'the door is always open in either direction'. She and I will make a clear ending to our present period of work together. If there comes a time in the future when she wants to open up a new area of change for herself, she can contact me again if she wishes to. At that time she and I can start afresh, exploring whether we are able and willing to enter into a new contract.

Criteria for Termination

You know that change means movement out of script and into autonomy. Yet no one ever becomes totally script-free. Nobody is autonomous one hundred per cent of the time. So on what criteria can you decide when to terminate?

Contract completion

Since virtually all TA practice is contractual, there is a sense in which the completion of a contract is always a minimum requirement for termination. However, contract completion can mean a great many different things. Your contract may be for some relatively minor behavioural change. At the other extreme, the client may complete contracts that entail redeciding major parts of his script. Either of these extremes, or any gradation between them, may be appropriate. It depends what your client wants and what you are willing to work with.

Berne: Four Phases of 'Cure'

Eric Berne (1961, 1972) proposed that there are four phases of cure:

- social control
- symptomatic relief
- transference cure
- script cure.

He suggested that these four types of cure would follow roughly in sequence during the process of change.

Social control

We say that a person exerts *social control* when she takes charge of her actions, engaging less often in scripty behaviour and increasing her use of autonomous behaviours. The person can achieve social control without necessarily altering any of her parental messages or resolving any of the unmet needs she may carry from her childhood.

To say this in terms of ego-states: social control means that the client takes control of her behaviour from Adult, even though the content of Parent and Child may remain unchanged.

Symptomatic relief

At the second stage, that of *symptomatic relief*, the client is not simply keeping Adult control of his scripty behaviours, but has begun to make changes in Child or Parent so that he feels less inclined to engage in these behaviours. For an increasing amount of the time he is solving problems without getting into script at all.

Transference cure

In transference cure, the client in Child has come to view the counsellor as a substitute for the client's original parent. Since the new 'parent' is giving more positive messages than the original one, the client can gain increased relief. If termination takes place at this stage, the client will have to arrange to 'keep the counsellor around' in his head, in the same way as he previously kept his original parent around.

Script cure

In his earlier writing (1961), Berne spoke of 'psychoanalytic cure' when describing the fourth and most complete stage of cure. Later, when he was developing his own theory of life-script, he changed the phrase to *script cure* (Berne, 1972). This entails the fundamental changes in the Child ego-state, with Adult support, that we met in Chapter 10 under the name of *redecision*. If script cure is achieved, the client can sustain his movement out of script even when the counsellor's support is withdrawn on termination.

Berne's four suggested phases of 'cure' can be seen as representing increasing degrees of movement out of the script. (If we think back to the description of the Racket System in Chapter 3: Berne's stage of 'social control' corresponds closely to what we there called 'interrupting the Racket System', while 'script cure' translates as 'breaking free from the Racket System'.) I am sure most transactional analysts would greatly prefer their clients to achieve script cure rather than terminate at the stages of symptomatic relief or transference cure. In fact, as you will realize from Chapter 10, one of the aims of the redecision approach is to eliminate the stage of transference cure altogether.

But sometimes the scope for change is limited by available time or resources. The client may be entirely satisfied to stop when he has achieved one of these less complete stages of cure. As always, contractual agreement is the key.

Erskine: Six Stages of Change

Richard Erskine (1973) has suggested that there are six stages of change which the client can be expected to go through in treatment. The stages are as follows:

1   Defensive.
2   Angry.
3   Hurt.
4   Recognizing self as problem.

5 Taking responsibility for change.
6 Forgiving the parents.

These stages are intended as a flexible guide only. One or more stages may be revisited if the client wishes to strengthen her change in these areas.

Stage 1: Defensive

At the initial *defensive* stage, the client will seek to defend both his own maladaptive patterns and those of his parents. He may typically say: 'Doesn't everybody act (feel) the way I do (the way my parents did)?' Feeling that these old patterns are at least familiar, he may still not be sure of his motivation for change.

Stage 2: Angry

Moving to the *angry* stage, the client becomes conscious of the ways in which he has been limiting himself by following outdated childhood strategies. He realizes too that these can be traced back to childhood desires that were not met, and he responds by becoming angry at his parents.

Stage 3: Hurt

Having experienced and expressed his held anger, the client is likely now to get in contact with the *hurt* he still feels over the needs he did not get met in childhood. At this stage it is the parents who are seen in a positive light, while the client experiences himself negatively. As he achieves increasing insight into the origins of his present problems, he may seek to leave counselling. However, insight is not the same as change, and termination at this stage is likely to be premature.

Stage 4: Recognizing self as problem

At the fourth stage, *recognition of self as problem*, the client becomes aware that it was he who chose the childhood patterns of behaviour that he is still replaying. With this realization comes a recognition of his own responsibility for his current problems. Again at this stage, the client may seek to terminate prematurely. This is because he may be experiencing fear in Child as he becomes more fully aware of the changes he can now make.

Stage 5: Taking responsibility for change

If the client stays in counselling, he is likely to move to the stage of *taking responsibility* for change. His self-statement now is: 'I don't need to keep on repeating old, painful behaviours.' With this, he owns his contract for change and takes self-motivated action to achieve it.

Stage 6: Forgiving the parents

At the final stage, the client extends *forgiveness to the parents*, saying to himself: 'My parents did the best job they were capable of doing.' By doing so, he also frees himself finally of the need to keep his parents around. 'Parents' here means primarily the internal Parents the client has constructed for himself. He may also become reconciled with his actual parents if they are still alive.

If you have a sense that something is incomplete about your work with a client, you may find it useful to make a mental check through Erskine's stages. For example, perhaps the client has expressed held anger at a parent-figure and gone on immediately to specify some changes she intends to make in behaviour. However, she then finds it difficult to make these behavioural changes. This may be because she has not yet allowed herself to feel hurt about childhood needs that the parent did not meet. Until she has experienced and expressed this feeling, she is likely to use energy in 'keeping the Parent around' internally rather than in making the grown-up changes she desires.

Woollams: Redecision and Response to Stress

When someone gets into script, she usually does so in response to stress. Stanley Woollams (1980) has used this fact to develop the concept of a *stress scale*. He builds upon the observation that redecision is not a matter of 'either/or'. Instead, the person redecides to a greater or lesser degree. Woollams suggests that the greater the degree of redecision, the greater the level of stress the person will be able to withstand without going into script.

Woollams does not formulate his 'stress scale' in terms that are objectively measurable, but you may find it a useful subjective idea to use in treatment and in deciding termination. The very concept of a *scale* of change can help both you and your client be clearly aware that nobody can ever change perfectly. What is possible instead is for the client to achieve an increasing degree of change. This can be gauged, suggests Woollams, by the client's increasing ability to stay out of script when under stress.

There is likely to come a time when the client feels he has developed enough of this ability. For sure, he might always achieve an even higher degree of redecision by staying in counselling. But this extra possible gain will no longer seem important enough to him to justify the extra expenditure of time and money that would be required to achieve it. When this trade-off point is reached, and agreed from Adult by both you and your client, you may judge it a sound reason to terminate.

John: Ending Counselling

You will remember from Chapter 5 that John and I agreed initially that we would meet for ten sessions. We would use the tenth of these for assessment of results and possible extension of our business contract.

In the event we decided to continue for a further ten sessions, with a review towards the end of that time. At session eighteen we discussed termination. We reached the mutual decision that session twenty would be our last.

During session nineteen I asked John if he would take an assignment to prepare a summary of the changes he had made during counselling, and bring this to the closing session. He did so, and we used it as the basis for a final debrief.

John's work: an overview

It seemed to us both that the turning-point in John's work had been the session in which he closed the escape hatches. You will recall from Chapter 7 that he was not willing to do this until session eleven, even though I had raised the possibility with him six sessions earlier. In the intervening sessions he had agreed to time-limited closure of the hatches.

When John came into session twelve, he reported to me that he had given up smoking. He had done this without any specific request from me. Indeed, he had not planned beforehand that he was going to do it, and he did not feel it had required any particular willpower. By the end of our work together he had still not smoked another cigarette. I interpreted this as meaning that John's Adult commitment not to harm self had already been 'heard' by him in Child, and that he had made a spontaneous move to redecide his early decision I Mustn't Exist. (I wish I could add here that closing the escape hatches has a similar immediate result for every smoker. Unfortunately, it does not.)

In session twelve also, John took the overall treatment contract concerning 'getting close to others' that I described in Chapter 8. You will recall that the behavioural marker we agreed upon in session twelve was that John would take time to listen to his girlfriend and tell her how he was feeling in response. In the following two sessions, he took two more behavioural contracts to further his overall goal. One was to share with his parents how he felt about them (session thirteen). The other was to be open with Helen about his fear that she might leave him and tell her he wanted her to stay with him (session fourteen).

I next decided to invite John into redecision work, and he agreed. In session fifteen he completed the two-chair exchange with his father that I have presented at length in Chapter 10. By closing escape hatches, John had already taken the Adult commitment not to harm others. Now he was also making the Child decision that he would ask for his needs to be met without using violence. Throughout the remaining sessions he continued behavioural practice of his redecision.

In session seventeen I asked John to place his parents and parent-figures, one by one, on another cushion in imagination. I invited him to assert to each one in turn that, whatever happened, he was going to stay alive and healthy, was going to let others stay alive and healthy, and was going to stay sane. (This is the positively phrased Child counterpart of the Adult undertaking to close escape hatches.) John did so. As he spoke to his 'mother', John first got in touch with furious rage, which he released by beating up the cushion. Next he shifted into terror as he re-experienced his early fear that his 'mother' might now go away and leave him totally abandoned. As he brought his here-and-now resources into this experience, John told his 'mother' 'I can survive without you'. Here, the word 'can' was not a let-out. His script belief had been that he *could not* survive without keeping his mother around. With this piece of work, John was re-visiting and strengthening the redecision to exist that he had already begun to make by session twelve.

At session eighteen John reported: 'My friends say I'm looking different – healthier and more relaxed.' I could also see this change in him and confirmed to him that I could. This was a further indication to both of us that he had made effective redecisions. He said he was continuing his practice of asking his girlfriend openly for what he wanted instead of getting aggressive with her. Helen, to judge by John's reports, was still adjusting to this new behaviour. She both welcomed it and did not quite know what to make of it. At times she invited John back into their familiar scripty exchanges. Though he still sometimes felt flashes of anger in response, he did so less intensely and less often than before. He had not used physical violence against Helen at any time since he entered counselling, and felt confident that he would not do so in future.

John said he was sure he wanted to stay in a permanent relationship with Helen. In session nineteen, he volunteered that he had come to like the idea of having a child with her. This, he said, was quite a change for him. Until now, he had regarded children as a nuisance and had certainly not thought of becoming a father himself.

His statement was a surprise for me also, and I did not know what to make of it at the time. After we had said our goodbyes at the end of session twenty, I speculated whether John's softening towards children also meant he had become more accepting of the Child in himself.

Postscript

A few weeks before I handed the manuscript of this book over to the publisher, I happened to be driving along a street in the town where I had worked with John. I looked out of the window of my car, and there was John walking along the pavement. He was wheeling a push-chair. In it was a young child.

I did not stop and hail John, so I do not know whether the infant in the push-chair was his and Helen's. But from what I could see, both John and the child seemed to be enjoying their walk.

REFERENCES

Allen, J. and B. Allen (1997) 'A New Type of Transactional Analysis and One Version of Script Work with a Constructionst Sensibility', *Transactional Analysis Journal*, 27(2): 89–98.

American Psychiatric Association (2000) *DSM-IV-TR (Diagnostic and Statistical Manual of Mental Disorders)* (fourth edition, text revision). Washington: American Psychiatric Association.

Bandler, R. and J. Grinder (1975) *The Structure of Magic*. I. Palo Alto: Science and Behaviour Books.

Barnes, G. (1977) 'Introduction', pp. 3–31 in G. Barnes (ed.), *Transactional Analysis After Eric Berne*. New York: Harper's College Press.

Berne, E. (1961) *Transactional Analysis in Psychotherapy*. New York: Grove Press.

Berne, E. (1964a) *Games People Play*. New York: Grove Press.

Berne, E. (1964b) 'Trading Stamps', *Transactional Analysis Bulletin*, 3(10): 127.

Berne, E. (1966) *Principles of Group Treatment*. New York: Oxford University Press.

Berne, E. (1972) *What Do You Say After You Say Hello?* New York: Grove Press.

Boliston-Mardula, J. (2001) 'Appetite Path Model: Working with Escape Hatch Resolution with Clients who Use Drugs and Alcohol', *TA UK*, 61 (Autumn): 9–14.

Bowlby, J. (1969) *Attachment and Loss*, Vol. 1: 'Attachment'. Harmondsworth: Penguin.

Boyd, H. (1976) 'The Structure and Sequence of Psychotherapy', *Transactional Analysis Journal*, 6(2): 180–3.

Boyd, H. and L. Cowles-Boyd (1980) 'Blocking Tragic Scripts', *Transactional Analysis Journal*, 10(3): 227–9.

Clarkson, P. (1987) 'Metaperspectives on Diagnosis', *Institute of Transactional Analysis News*, 18 (Winter): 6–11.

Clarkson, P. (1989) *Gestalt Counselling in Action*. London: Sage.

Clarkson, P. (1992) *Transactional Analysis Psychotherapy: An Integrated Approach*. London: Routledge.

Cornell, W. (1986) 'Setting the Therapeutic Stage: The Initial Sessions', *Transactional Analysis Journal*, 16(1): 4–10.

Cornell, W. and H. Hargaden (2005) *From Transactions to Relations: The Emergence of a Relational Tradition in Transactional Analysis*. Chadlington: Haddon Press.

Cornell, W. and N. Landaiche (2006) 'Impasse and Intimacy: Applying Berne's Concept of Script Protocol', *Transactional Analysis Journal*, 36(3): 196–213.

Cowles-Boyd, L. (1980) 'Psychosomatic Disturbances and Tragic Script Payoffs', *Transactional Analysis Journal*, 10(3): 230–1.

Crossman, P. (1966) 'Permission and Protection', *Transactional Analysis Bulletin*, 5(19): 152–4.

Drye, R. (2006) 'The No-Suicide Decision: Then and Now', *The Script*, 36(6): 3–4. (Reprinted in *Insititute of Transactional Analysis News*, 27 (October 2006): 1–6.)

Drye, R., R. Goulding and M. Goulding (1973) 'No-Suicide Decisions: Patient Monitoring of Suicidal Risk', *American Journal of Psychiatry*, 130(2): 118–21.

Dusay, J. (1966) 'Response to Games in Therapy', *Transactional Analysis Bulletin*, 5(18): 136–7.

English, F. (1971) 'The Substitution Factor: Rackets and Real Feelings', *Transactional Analysis Journal*, 1(4): 225–30.

English, F. (1972) 'Rackets and Real Feelings, Part II', *Transactional Analysis Journal*, 2(1): 23–5.

English, F. (1976a) 'Racketeering', *Transactional Analysis Journal*, 6(1): 78–81.

English, F. (1976b) 'Differentiating Victims in the Drama Triangle', *Transactional Analysis Journal*, 6(4): 384–6.

English, F. (1977) 'What Shall I Do Tomorrow? Reconceptualizing Transactional Analysis', pp. 287–347 in G. Barnes (ed.), *Transactional Analysis After Eric Berne*. New York: Harper's College Press.

Erikson, E. (1950) *Childhood and Society*. New York: W.W. Norton.

Erskine, R. (1973) 'Six Stages of Treatment', *Transactional Analysis Journal*, 3(3): 17–18.

Erskine, R. (1980) 'Script Cure: Behavioral, Intrapsychic and Physiological', *Transactional Analysis Journal*, 10(2): 102–6.

Erskine, R. (1991) 'Transference and Transactions: Critique from an Intrapsychic and Integrative Perspective', *Transactional Analysis Journal*, 21(2): 63–76.

Erskine, R. and J. Moursund (1988) *Integrative Psychotherapy in Action*. Newbury Park, CA: Sage.

Erskine, R. and M. Zalcman (1979) 'The Racket System: A Model for Racket Analysis', *Transactional Analysis Journal*, 9(1): 51–9.

Fisch, R., J. Weakland and L. Segal (1982) *The Tactics of Change: Doing Therapy Briefly*. San Francisco, CA: Jossey-Bass.

Gobes, L. (1985) 'Abandonment and Engulfment: Issues in Relationship Therapy', *Transactional Analysis Journal*, 15(3): 216–19.

Goulding, M. and R. Goulding (1979) *Changing Lives Through Redecision Therapy*. New York: Brunner/Mazel.

Goulding, R. (1977) 'No Magic at Mt. Madonna: Redecisions in Marathon Therapy', pp. 77–95 in G. Barnes (ed.), *Transactional Analysis After Eric Berne*. New York: Harper's College Press.

Goulding, R. (1985) 'History of Redecision Therapy', pp. 9–10 in L. Kadis (ed.), *Redecision Therapy: Expanded Perspectives*. Watsonville, CA: Western Institute for Group and Family Therapy.

Goulding, R. and M. Goulding (1972) 'New Directions in Transactional Analysis', pp. 105–34 in C. Sager and H. Kaplan (eds), *Progress in Group and Family Therapy*. New York: Brunner/Mazel.

Goulding, R. and M. Goulding (1976) 'Injunctions, Decisions and Redecisions', *Transactional Analysis Journal*, 6(1): 41–8.

Goulding, R. and M. Goulding (1978) *The Power is in the Patient*. San Francisco, CA: TA Press.

Guichard, M. (1987) 'Writing the Long Case Study', workshop presentation, EATA Conference, Chamonix (unpublished).

Haykin, M. (1980) 'Type Casting: The Influence of Early Childhood upon the Structure of the Child Ego-State', *Transactional Analysis Journal*, 10(4): 354–64.

James, J. (1976) 'Positive Payoffs after Games', *Transactional Analysis Journal*, 6(3): 259–62.

Joines, V. (1982) 'Similarities and Differences in Rackets and Games', *Transactional Analysis Journal*, 12(4): 280–3.

Joines, V. and I. Stewart (2002) *Personality Adaptations: A New Guide to Human Understanding in Psychotherapy and Counselling*. Nottingham and Chapel Hill, NC: Lifespace.

Kadis, L. (ed.) (1985) *Redecision Therapy: Expanded Perspectives*. Watsonville, CA: Western Institute for Group and Family Therapy.

Klein, J. (1987) *Our Need for Others and its Roots in Infancy*. London: Tavistock.

Levine, S. (1960) 'Stimulation in Infancy', *Scientific American*, 202(5): 80–6.

McNeel, J. (1976) 'The Parent Interview', *Transactional Analysis Journal*, 6(1): 61–8.

Mearns, D. and B. Thorne (2007) *Person-Centred Counselling in Action* (2nd edn published 1999). London: Sage.

Mellor, K. (1979) 'Suicide: Being Killed, Killing and Dying', *Transactional Analysis Journal*, 9(3): 182–8.

Mellor, K. (1980a) 'Impasses: A Developmental and Structural Understanding', *Transactional Analysis Journal*, 10(3): 213–22.

Mellor, K. (1980b) 'Reframing and the Integrated Use of Redeciding and Reparenting', *Transactional Analysis Journal*, 10(3): 204–13.

Mellor, K. and E. Sigmund (1975a) 'Discounting', *Transactional Analysis Journal*, 5(3): 295–302.

Mellor, K. and E. Sigmund (1975b) 'Redefining', *Transactional Analysis Journal*, 5(3): 303–11.

Mothersole, G. (2006) 'Contracts and Harmful Behaviour', pp. 87–97 in C. Sills (ed.), *Contracts in Counselling and Psychotherapy* (2nd edn). London: Sage.

Moursund, J. and R. Erskine (2004) *Integrative Psychotherapy: The Art and Science of Relationship*. Belmont, CA: Wadsworth.

Novellino, M. (2005) 'Transactional Psychoanalysis: Epistemological Foundations', *Transactional Analysis Journal*, 35(2): 157–72.

Perls, F. (1971) *Gestalt Therapy Verbatim*. Des Plaines, IL: Bantam.

Perls, F. (1976) *The Gestalt Approach and Eyewitness to Therapy*. Des Plaines, IL: Bantam.

Piaget, J. (1951) *The Child's Conception of the World*. London: Routledge and Kegan Paul.

Pulleyblank, E. and P. McCormick (1985) 'The Stages of Redecision Therapy', pp. 51–9 in L. Kadis (ed.), *Redecision Therapy: Expanded Perspectives*. Watsonville, CA: Western Institute for Group and Family Therapy.

Rogers, C. (1961) *On Becoming a Person: A Therapist's View of Psychotherapy*. London: Constable.

Rowan, J. (1981) 'Diagnosis', *Self and Society*, 9(4): 153–60.

Ruppert, E. (1986) 'Relationships and Script Transformation' (unpublished).

Scheflen, A. (1972) *Body Language and Social Order*. Englewood Cliffs, NJ: Prentice-Hall.

Schiff, J., A. Schiff, K. Mellor, E. Schiff, J. Fishman, L. Wolz, C. Fishman and D. Momb (1975) *The Cathexis Reader: Transactional Analysis Treatment of Psychosis*. New York: Harper and Row.

Sills, C. (ed.) (2006) *Contracts in Counselling and Psychotherapy* (2nd edn). London: Sage.

Sills, C. and H. Hargaden (eds) (2003) *Ego States*. London: Worth Publishing.

Spitz, R. (1945) 'Hospitalism: Genesis of Psychiatric Conditions in Early Childhood', *Psychoanalytic Studies of the Child*, 1: 53–74.

Steere, D. (1982) *Bodily Expressions in Psychotherapy*. New York: Brunner/Mazel.

Steiner, C. (1966) 'Script and Counterscript', *Transactional Analysis Bulletin*, 5(18): 133–5.

Steiner, C. (1974) *Scripts People Live: Transactional Analysis of Life Scripts*. New York: Grove Press.

Stewart, I. (1987) 'Time-Frames, Theory and Therapy', audiotape of workshop presentation, ITAA Conference, Chicago. Hobart: Repeat Performance Tapes.

Stewart, I. (1992) *Key Figures in Counselling and Psychotherapy: Eric Berne*. London: Sage.

Stewart, I. (1996a) *Developing Transactional Analysis Counselling*. London: Sage.

Stewart, I. (1996b) 'The Development of Transactional Analysis', in W. Dryden (ed.), *Development of Psychotherapy: Historical Perspectives*. London: Sage.

Stewart, I. (2001) 'Closing Escape Hatches: Always Therapeutic, Never Routine', *TA UK*, 60, Summer (reprinted in *The Script*, 31(4), May 2001).

Stewart, I. (2006) 'Outcome-Focused Contracts', pp. 63–73 in C. Sills, (ed.), *Contracts in Counselling and Psychotherapy* (2nd edn). London: Sage.

Stewart, I. and V. Joines (1987) *TA Today: A New Introduction to Transactional Analysis*. Nottingham and Chapel Hill, NC: Lifespace.

Summers, G. and K. Tudor (2000) 'Co-creative Transactional Analysis', *Transactional Analysis Journal*, 30(1): 23–40.

Szasz, T. (1961) *The Myth of Mental Illness*. New York: Harper and Row.

Thomson, G. (1983) 'Fear, Anger and Sadness', *Transactional Analysis Journal*, 13(1): 20–4.

Tilney, T. (1998) *Dictionary of Transactional Analysis*. London: Whurr Publishers.

Transactional Analysis Journal (1980) 10(2), Symposium Issue on 'Cure'.

Ware, P. (1983) 'Personality Adaptations', *Transactional Analysis Journal*, 13(1): 11–19.

White, J. and T. White (1975) 'Cultural Scripting', *Transactional Analysis Journal*, 5(1): 12–23.

Woollams, S. (1977) 'From 21 to 43', pp. 351–93 in G. Barnes (ed.), *Transactional Analysis After Eric Berne*. New York: Harper's College Press.

Woollams, S. (1980) 'Cure!?', *Transactional Analysis Journal*, 10(2): 115–17.

Woollams, S. and M. Brown (1978) *Transactional Analysis*. Dexter: Huron Valley Institute.

Zalcman, M. (1986) 'Racket Analysis and the Racket System', workshop presentation, EATA Conference, Noordwijkerhout (unpublished).

Zalcman, M. (1987) 'Game Analysis and Racket Analysis', pp. 11–14 in *Keynote Speeches Delivered at the EATA Conference, July 1986*. Geneva: European Association for Transactional Analysis.

Zigler, E. and L. Phillips (1961) 'Psychiatric Diagnosis: A Critique', *Journal of Abnormal and Social Psychology*, 63: 607–8.

INDEX